Advance Praise for

Pursuing Purpose

This is a well-crafted, gentle, and honest sharing of Dent Gitchel's spiritual journey to discovering his core values and what is most life giving for him. He invites us to follow our own heart's deepest longings and to embark on our personal spiritual journey. His hope is that we too can find that space within that is home to our true selves. Dent does not sugarcoat the doubts or other obstacles to be found on this path. But, like the Buddha, he wants to alleviate suffering where it exists, invites us to come and see, and try for ourselves what he has found to be true. This first book for author Dent Gitchel garners well-deserved kudos.

—**Sharon Salzberg**,
author of *Lovingkindness* and *Real Change*

Dent Gitchel has written a heartfelt, personal and extremely useful guide to meditation which helps to bridge the gap between ancient wisdom and modern experience.

—**Ethan Nichtern**, Author, Buddhist Teacher

Dent Gitchel's *Pursuing Purpose* speaks to the courage and compassion that is our birthright, urging us to cultivate awareness in the warm, familiar, and patient voice of a long-sought-for kalyāṇa-mitta: the spiritual friend that Buddha said was an essential companion when learning to navigate the road of life and death. An excellent introduction to practice for beginners, *Pursuing Purpose* will also reawaken the mind of the seeker in seasoned meditators. I'm grateful for this book.

—**Steve Silberman**, Author, *NeuroTribes: The Legacy of Autism and the Future of Neurodiversity*

Where was this book 50 years ago, when I first got interested in spirituality? *Pursuing Purpose* is a life companion. The metaphor used in this book of coming home is so apt. As a younger spiritual seeker, I had to come to grips with my desire to flee from experience, and now working with students I see this yet again.

Dent Gitchel's introduction to the well-considered life amply addresses the folly of such an avoidant stance. Many of us drawn to spirituality carry ample baggage of self-recrimination and desires to escape. In a most considerate and compassionate manner, *Pursuing Purpose* invites us to the fully lived life—to come home to ourselves. Amen! Over and over, in a manner that is most supportive, the author cautions against the ever-lurking danger of using personal guidance for growth as an opportunity for self-criticism. This is so helpful.

This book does not promise pie-in-the-sky, or idealized results. Rather, it offers gentle suggestions to a densely enriched fully dimensional human life. Stocked with many instructions for self-reflection, meditation, journaling, and bringing one's values into daily life, this book can serve as a Google map for our lives.

I recommend this book most highly both to the new and seasoned seekers of a meaning-rich life, wanting to learn how to meditate or enhance it, and those wanting a value-guided healthy relationship with their emotions, and others. This book is most of all a kind, gentle, encouragement to deepen our emotional and spiritual self-understanding not through closing our eyes to any aspect of life but rather through full acknowledgment of our very humanity.

—**Harvey B. Aronson**, PhD, LCSW, LMFT, LCDC,
Co-Founder, Dawn Mountain Center for Tibetan Buddhism

I love the power and clarity of this book. Based on 30 years as a practitioner, professional, and expert, the author distinguishes *Wholesome Mindfulness* as a powerful new path that you can trust. With precision and wisdom Dent Gitchel walks with you step by step through "coming home to your place in the world and taking the lead in your life." Along the way he generously shares from his heart to yours. The result is the curiosity, courage, and confidence to engage in the messiness of life and the word in new, wiser and more resilient ways. This book is recommended for anyone enduring the crises of modern life and looking for lasting relief.

—**Monica Hanson**,
Founding Faculty of Stanford's Compassion Cultivation Training and Co-Founder and Director of the Applied Compassion Training (ACT) and Academy hosted by the Center for Compassion at Stanford University

At times when even the wealthiest societies are facing turmoil and systemic crisis at unprecedented levels, most of us are feeling the urge to reorder our priorities and rethink how we want to live as a person and as a species. For this challenging process of finding and expressing what is truly meaningful and cultivating a mind and a heart that are helpful for self and others, I heartfully recommend the gentle and wise guidance of Dent Gitchel in *Pursuing Purpose*. From his own several decades of sincere personal search, the author distills in this book the kind of simple and profound advice that only a good spiritual friend can offer.

—**Gonzalo Brito Pons**, PhD,
Director of the Compassion Cultivation Training (CCT) Teacher Training Program for Spanish-speaking countries, Co-Author of *The Mindfulness-Based Emotional Balance Workbook* and *Presencia Plena: Reflexiones y Prácticas para Cultivar Mindfulness en la Vida Diaria*

The warm and gentle wisdom of Wholesome Mindfulness reminds me not only why to live a life of purpose, but it gives hands-on approaches for how to get there. Through storytelling, journaling exercises, meditation, and real-world practices, this book helps me tap into my inner goodness and be a more courageous, conscious, compassionate, and values-driven human. This is a perfect book for seekers, whether experienced in meditation or not.

—**Sara Schairer**, Founder of Compassion It™

Mindfulness, so popularly stripped down to a form of awareness, is presented here as intrinsically and deeply tied to our capacity for courage, emotional authenticity, and our unique sense of what values make life most worth living. Dr. Gitchel weaves together his years of teaching, contemplative practice, scholarship, and deep-hearted wisdom to build a practical, stepwise guide back to the self you were born to be. A necessary light for a time darkened by societal divisions and isolation.

—**Matthew D. Skinta**, PhD, ABPP,
Assistant Professor of Psychology, Roosevelt University

Being connected to a sense of purpose and meaning is one of the most important things we can cultivate to build resilience and emotional balance. *Pursuing Purpose* is, a persuasive, clarifying account of how contemplative practices such as meditation, mindfulness, journaling, and simply pausing to reflect help motivate us to identify and act towards the things that matter the most. *Pursuing Purpose* banishes any biases about meditation or mindful practices being primarily to achieve states of relaxation. It inspires and motivates us to reflect on deeper values and principles that are affecting our everyday actions, life directions, and engagement with community.

—**Laurisa Dill**, M.Ed.,
Registered Psychotherapist, Mindful Leadership Trainer,
Consultant and Founder of Mindful Momentum

Pursuing Purpose isn't just another book on meditation; it offers practices for mind, body, and spirit for those who are longing to "come home" to our deepest selves. It gives us a form of mindfulness that's oriented toward cultivating a more wholesome life, from the subtle level of thoughts to the more obvious ways we interact with society. If you've been waiting for a wise friend to walk you through the beginnings of real meditation practice, you're in luck: With down-to-earth instructions and a caring tone, *Pursuing Purpose* is here for you.

—**Claire Villarreal**, PhD, Author and Meditation Teacher

Pursuing Purpose provides what many have been seeking for a long time: a brief, concise, and practical guide to meditation. But it is far more than a simple guide to sitting down and quieting the mind. It is at once a spiritual autobiography, a field guide to contemplative thought, a penetrating commentary on contemporary society, a workbook, and perhaps most importantly, a reliable and authoritative friend to help you along the path of "coming home." Whether you are an experienced mindfulness practitioner or a curious novice who wants to know more about this activity called meditation, *Pursuing Purpose* will provide you with the information—the wisdom, really—that you need to live compassionately and with an ever-evolving sense of your own happiness and your responsibility to the community that allows you to pursue it. I can't recommend this book highly enough.

—**Sidney Burris**, PhD,
Professor, Department of English, University of Arkansas,
Co-Founder, Tibetan Cultural Institute of Arkansas

Pursuing Purpose

A Guide To Finding Meaning Through Meditation

DENT GITCHEL JR., PhD

modern wisdom
PRESS

Modern Wisdom Press, Boulder, Colorado, USA

www.modernwisdompress.com

Published 2020

Cover Design: Jennifer Miles

Author's photo courtesy of Lindsey Sullivan

For my children, Lilah and Henry, and my wife Shannon.
You have taught me
how to Love and be Loved.
To all of my teachers,
Without you, I would not have found myself,
and would have nothing to give.
To my parents and grandparents and ancestors,
You laid the foundation for all that I have become.
To all current and future inhabitants of planet Earth,
May we flourish together in compassion, kindness,
and harmony, and learn to value
All of life and creation.

Contents

Foreword

I was born into a world much different than the contemporary modern world. Leaving Tibet as a small child, and spending my childhood in India, I never dreamed that I would someday live in the United States. Yet, I settled in Fayetteville, Arkansas, in 2006. I met Dent Gitchel in the first class that I taught at the University of Arkansas, and he has remained my friend and student since then.

Tibetan history is an extraordinary blend of conquest and retreat, but when Indian philosophy arrived in Tibet around the 7th century, the country, under the enlightened leadership of three successive kings, gradually withdrew from the Asian world stage and began to cultivate science of the mind.

This period of time, from the 7th through the 19th centuries, saw the rise in Western Europe and America of a fully equipped technological society, culminating in the exploration of outer space. In Tibet, during the same time, technology was ignored in favor of exploring what the Dalai Lama likes to call "inner space." Since then Tibetan culture has been deeply infused into modern science by cultivating ancient spiritual elements of science of the mind. Indian master Dharmakirti suggests that, unlike physical abilities, the qualities of the mind have the potential for limitless development. If we understand that the essential nature of consciousness (mind) is neutral, we can begin to comprehend that change is possible.

Moreover, if one creates the right conditions of mindfulness and meditation one can consciously direct change to transformation of the state of mind. Within the domain of the emotions, there might be a family consisting of negative emotions, like hate, anger, hostility, and so forth, while in opposition is a family of positive emotions, like mindfulness and meditation, love, and compassion. So if one works to increase, reinforce, and strengthen the positive groups, one will correspondingly weaken the negative ones, thus effectively bringing about transformation in one's thoughts and emotions and life.

Dent is a very sincere student of meditation and has a great knack for being able to explain things in ways that resonate with others. This is a very important skill because as mindfulness and meditation become more popular, there is a danger that depth and authenticity will be forsaken in the favor of simplicity and accessibility. It is important to be able to explain the techniques and benefits of meditation in ways that inspire modern persons but that do not water down the spiritual roots of the mindfulness movement.

Dent has done a masterful job of presenting meditation practices in ways that are useful to modern persons, while also respecting the depth and sophistication of these practices. This is not a Buddhist book. It is part of the secular mindfulness meditation movement that has provided comfort and sustenance to countless individuals. Yet, it is very important to remember and honor the spiritual roots of mindfulness. This book does exactly that. It presents meditation practices and perspectives in accessible and modern ways while not abandoning their spiritual depth and orientation.

By emphasizing a value-based orientation and a gradual progression of practices, this book may serve as a practical resource to both beginners and seasoned practitioners on the path of meditation. It is full of heartfelt advice and suggestions for cultivating a contemplative life in the busy world. Readers are offered a series of guided meditations, short practices, and strategies for navigating life with purpose.

The modern world is very complex and interconnected. People come from a wide variety of cultural and religious backgrounds. As we celebrate this diversity, it is also important to cultivate an attitude of compassion, tolerance, and goodwill. In a pluralistic world, a secular-based approach to ethics is very important, and *Pursuing Purpose* is an important contribution.

This book can serve as a friendly guide and companion on the path of life. It is a concise and heartfelt manual for cultivating a contemplative approach to life in the modern world. It is my hope that many will benefit from it.

—**Geshe Thupten Dorjee**, Faculty, ARSC Humanities Program, University of Arkansas, Co-Founder, Tibetan Cultural Institute of Arkansas

Introduction

Life is challenging. Even with the most well-laid plans, challenges and obstacles emerge, and it is up to each of us to navigate the shifting currents of reality. We all are tasked with forging a journey of our own. This book is written to help you on your journey through the practices of *Wholesome Mindfulness*.

Mindfulness is a tool. It is essentially about waking up to the present and to what is actually occurring. It is about training yourself to be in the present moment, with curiosity and without distraction. However, as a technique, it is value-neutral. Like any tool, its benefits depend on the purposes to which it is used. For instance, mindfulness can be successfully employed to perform better in sports or academics. It is a tool—a technique—that can be learned and applied to many contexts.

However, it was originally developed and implemented in spiritual traditions emphasizing personal transformation. The guidance within this book is consistent to this latter approach but intended to help modern people to develop more purpose, meaning, and compassion—thus, the term "wholesome." What is wholesome nourishes, and a wholesome approach to mindfulness nourishes a meaningful life. When we approach our life from this perspective, we are guided by meaning and purpose and these are fused into all of our activities and relationships. *Wholesome Mindfulness*, then, helps to foster a meaningful and intentional approach to life.

As someone with three decades of meditation experience, and ten years' experience helping others to meditate, this book is from my heart to yours. If you are looking for perfection, this book is not for you. This book is not about perfection. It is about life. Your life is your life and yours alone, and whatever brings you to these pages is authentic. My hope is that this book, at least in some small way, can help you find what you need to achieve lasting happiness, purpose, and contentment. I envision a day in which you are able to live according to your deepest values and wishes, and in which your deepest fears and confusions may be overcome. This book is my offering to you.

The Dissatisfied Mind

We all come to meditation for different reasons, yet a majority of us arrive on our cushion due to underlying stress or a general sense of dissatisfaction. The ancient Greek philosopher Socrates said that "the unexamined life is not worth living." Likewise, ancient Buddhist psychology claims that the unexamined life is full of suffering. Neither of these, however, is a pessimistic view. Each point to a life of inquiry and ethics that addresses and overcomes a core discomfort of human existence. In modern life, the discomfort of human existence is often experienced as stress, anxiety, and lack of meaning.

The modern world presents unprecedented challenges. For one, our lives have become exceedingly busy. Modern emphases on productivity expect us to work more and to do more with less. Value is largely associated with production. Second, our minds have become increasingly inundated with information. Modes and types of communication evolve at dizzying rates. We live in a constant state of information overload. At almost all times, we are taking, sending, and receiving information. Moreover, we are treated largely as objects to be manipulated by the marketplace. The message of most advertising is that we are incomplete and can only be fulfilled by products or services. Fulfillment, however, never manifests. The more that we buy in to this mentality, the more that we continue to seek meaning in external goods or services, leading to repetitive cycles of searching for meaning.

Additionally, there are social and environmental challenges that threaten civilization as we know it—if not life itself—such as the global COVID-19 pandemic. Tribalism is on the rise, accompanied by the re-emergence of just about every other "ism" imaginable. Climate change, resource depletion, and overpopulation threaten our ecological sustainability. The threat of war and civil unrest hang over us at all times like dark clouds refusing to disperse. Income inequality manifests as a small portion of persons living in unparalleled and grotesque luxury, while others fight to survive and have a comfortable life, and the vast majority struggle to have even the most basic resources necessary for life. These large-scale challenges are overwhelming and can lead to distress.

It can be very difficult to find our way in this modern predicament. Do you sometimes experience anxiety about your life and your place in the world? Do you struggle with finding lasting meaning and purpose? Are you ever stressed or overwhelmed in the face of the responsibilities and unpredictability of life? Do you ever worry about who to believe in a world of mixed messages? If you answered yes to any or all of the above questions, then you are not alone. You, I, and countless others experience these symptoms of modernity. These symptoms manifest differently in each of our lives, but there is an underlying sense of shared dissatisfaction. However, this is not the end of the story.

Enter Wholesome Mindfulness

Our dissatisfaction can be a burden that never disappears, or it can become a stepping stone to help us transform our lives into paths of meaning and purpose. The dissatisfaction is a given. It is there without our asking and results from the particular characteristics of modern life. However, it is up to us how we *respond* to this dissatisfaction. The techniques of *Wholesome Mindfulness* help us to respond in healthy and deliberate ways emerging from a set of personal values grounded in a clear understanding of our own needs and of the needs of others around us.

This journey can become the most important journey that you will ever take. The practices of *Wholesome Mindfulness* can help you to access and cultivate inner resources, leading to more purpose and clarity and to less confusion and anxiety. This can lead to a more resilient and purposeful way of life.

That is ultimately what you will learn about in the next chapters of the book. *Wholesome Mindfulness* is about using the tools of mindfulness to help bring you back to the present moment, addressing your body, emotions, values, and relationships. It is here that you will find clarity and contentment. This is your birthright. It is everyone's birthright. The seeds are already within you; they simply need to be watered with nourishing, contemplative practices. You've got this!

How to Use this Book

How you use this book is up to you, but I have a few suggestions. First, it is best to read this book slowly but deliberately. It is not a long book, but there is a lot of depth here. You will learn strategies to get to know yourself better, to give yourself the love and support you need, and to develop a more wholesome attitude toward life. You will learn to tap into your innermost values and to express them, and to live from this core in your daily life. You will learn to focus and calm the mind, and to bring more awareness to your own thoughts and feelings, resulting in more freedom and choice in your life. You will learn to better navigate the terrain of your emotions and to become less reactive. You will learn to foster kindness for yourself and others. I call this process *coming home.*

Take your time and allow the information to digest and to provide nourishment.

Second, I advise keeping a journal—beginning now—to mindfully and reflectively record your experiences and observations about the material. And finally, I recommend engaging with the material and practices regularly, even if only for a few minutes at a time.

There are three types of practices offered in this book: (1) formal meditation practices, (2) self-reflective activities, and (3) embodied practices. There are formal meditation practices designed to be done in short sessions, typically 15–20 minutes. Guided audio meditations (along with additional practices and support for your journey) can be found at www.dentgitchel.com/pursuingpurpose. Self-reflective activities include journaling prompts to help you reflect upon your experience. Embodied practices are very brief mindfulness activities to be integrated into daily life. Though seemingly simple, these techniques are important for truly integrating the material into your daily life and sustaining lasting change. Each of these three foundations in the coming chapters reinforces the others and each is important in the development of a perspective of *Wholesome Mindfulness*. Much more will be said of these as we progress on this journey.

Section 1 of the book is preparatory. In any important endeavor, it is important to have a blueprint and a foundation. In Chapter 1, you'll see how particular symptoms of the modern mindset make the practices and perspectives of *Wholesome Mindfulness* important and vital. In Chapter 2, you'll learn about what gives meditation practices their power. In Chapter 3, you'll gain more detailed instructions on how to work with practices of *Wholesome Mindfulness* and contemplative practices in general.

Section 2 showcases the heart of the practices. Chapter 4 offers practices that help to come home to bodily sensations and to the present moment, as well as practices that help to tap into your innermost values. Chapter 5 introduces practices to engage what I call our Innate Goodness, the wise heart that wants the best both for ourselves and for others. Chapter 6 offers practices and perspectives that help us to deal with emotions, which is very critical for those of us living in the modern age. Our emotions are triggered countless times every day, and it is imperative to be able to recognize and work with them skillfully.

Section 3 widens the scope and offers strategies for fully embodying the practices and perspectives of Section 2 in the complex and messy modern world. Chapter 7 brings mindfulness into the physical, social, and virtual spaces that we inhabit. Chapter 8 furthers this process by bringing the loving capacities of the heart into the real relationships that we live and breathe in. Finally, Chapter 9 offers final reflections and strategies for working with the material as you move forward on your path.

Your Guide

I have been traversing the contemplative path for many years now. For various reasons, I questioned the conventional realities and the way they were presented to me by family and culture from a very young age. I have always been a seeker, and this has led me to explore many paths. I have gone down many a rabbit hole and have immersed myself in both ancient and contemporary spiritual teachings, drawing deep sustenance from popular culture as well. In 1990, I discovered formal meditation practice and the ancient teachings of Buddhism. In many ways, my life since then has been driven by attempts, both conscious and unconscious, to sort through these various influences and forge a meaningful and purpose-driven life in the modern world. Throughout these past three decades, meditation has served increasingly as the foundation of my life, and I have been fortunate to encounter many amazing teachers. Without them, I do not know if I would have found my own path home. My hope is that this book will assist you in your own journey home.

Part of the journey home, at least for me, is in wanting to help others on their own journeys home. An engaged, contemplative life can be powerfully transformative. It is natural to want to share this with others. I have taught in various spiritual and secular frameworks and have become increasingly interested in this emerging interface of contemplative practices and modern life. What contemplative practices are best suited for modern life? And, how best do we teach and implement them? I'm excited to share what I've learned and created through my *Wholesome Mindfulness* approach. Thank you for joining me on this journey.

Section 1

Coming Home from the Dissatisfied Mind

Chapter 1

The First Step on Your Journey

Coming Home

When we engage in *Wholesome Mindfulness* practices, we are waking up and coming home to what is best within us, even if it does not always feel that way. This journey may run directly counter to what you have been accustomed to doing. We are used to going *somewhere* and moving *toward* something. This manifests in many ways. Our culture has placed great value on busyness, productivity, and achievement. We are told: Do, do, do! Achieve, achieve, achieve! Certainly, these emphases have been beneficial on many levels. For example, the improvements in technology and quality of life (for some) are mind-boggling. For instance, I am writing this sentence from a laptop computer that was unimaginable in the not-too-distant past, while listening to my favorite music streamed from some mysterious "universe," with the knowledge base of the world literally at my fingertips!

The journey home is a different type of journey than one of productivity or achievement. The journey home connects us to inner resources and aspects of ourselves that are typically dormant or malnourished in the modern world. We are taught to do and to achieve, and to define ourselves in terms of external successes and failures, but are largely not taught how to *be with ourselves*. This manifests in different ways. For many, there is a lack of emotional awareness and literacy and difficulty being with strong and difficult emotions. There is a tendency toward distraction and a constant search for new stimulating forms of entertainment. And, there is often a deep inner sense of purposelessness. These might be consciously recognized, but for most of us they exist just below the surface of conscious awareness. In sum, I refer to these symptoms of modernity as the *dissatisfied mind.*

In modern society, as we focus on doing and achieving, our anxiety and dissatisfaction often increase. We may even lose the ability to relax in healthy ways. We may constantly feel just a little unsettled and uncertain of ourselves. We are left empty, drained, and perhaps confused. We might even become numb to who we really are. I know that I have suffered from all of this and continue to struggle with these symptoms of the modern world every day. We become lost, with only a vague sense that we are lost, and really no idea where home is. We are lost without a map. I call this the *cowardly self.* Fortunately, adopting a perspective of *Wholesome Mindfulness* can help lead us home, to a place of courage, confidence, and purpose. The *cowardly self* does not have the final say.

The *cowardly self* is not inherently problematic. Ultimately, it is there to protect us. It is tied to the ancient reptilian part of our brains and operates largely from the perspective of survival-based emotions and problem-solving. It is there to get us out of a bind and to do so quickly. This self emerges, along with the thoughts and emotions that accompany it, whenever we feel threatened. However, in the modern predicament, this mechanism gets triggered time and time again. We constantly feel bombarded and threatened by modern life and our *cowardly self* is always on guard and seeking solutions. This mechanism, which is critical in the face of direct threats, becomes the default mode of operating in all aspects of life. The result is anxiety, discontent, and constant self-evaluation. What evolved to protect us now manifests in ways that inhibit healthy functioning. Fortunately, however, this is not the end of the story.

The *cowardly self* operates largely out of fear and confusion. Because of this, we lose our way. But recognizing that we are lost is an important step. It is from here that the journey home begins. The *cowardly self* is alone and afraid, but the perspective practices of *Wholesome Mindfulness* provide clarity, confidence, and direction, and we begin to see that there is also a much broader perspective from which to live. It takes a lot of courage to hear and heed this call, and to begin to be with our experiences. For this reason, I call this the *courageous self.* If you are reading these words you already have this courage. It just needs to be further reinforced and recognized. Whereas the *cowardly self* is small, lost, frightened, and scared, the *courageous self* is expansive, content, and strong. The *courageous self* is your birthright, and this book will help you to live life more and more from its perspective. Coming home involves a journey to access meaning beyond productivity and entertainment to a state of relaxation and focus, and to our inner— perhaps undeveloped—positive qualities. A life of meaning and purpose is the outcome of this journey.

It takes courage to come home, and you already have this courage. Even if it is unrecognized or has never been validated by others, it is there. You will be cultivating your *courageous self* in this book. You will tap into and discover your true home and begin the journey back there. You may not feel that you have this courage, but you do. The path home is uniquely yours and yours alone, but there is a general and universal sense of goodness and courage that resides within us. It is both the destination and the path. Whereas the *cowardly self* has taken us further and further away from our true values, the *courageous* self leads us back to our true nature and purpose. The path home is there for the waiting.

The *courageous self* is brave because it does not succumb to the fears and anxieties of the *cowardly self.* It is able to forge ahead on the journey home and to discover aspects of personhood that have been underdeveloped or long buried. The journey home takes courage and strength because we come face to face with many deeply ingrained mental and emotional habits and may *choose* to relate to these in new and healthier ways. It takes courage because our moral compass becomes our own inner sense of ethics and direction. It takes courage because sometimes we are called to give up long-held beliefs and assumptions about ourselves and the world at large. The *courageous self* leads us on the journey home, and like any journey, there are risks and uncertainties. But there are also unexpected beauties, wonders, and meaningful discoveries. The journey home is largely a journey back to who you really are. Below are some of the terrains that will be traversed on this journey.

Coming Home to Your True Values

Sometimes I have had a fuzzy sense that something does not feel right or that something really does feel right. I have had a sense that some things fit who I really was and others did not, but could not articulate why. As the years have passed, and with the insights gained through meditation and study, I have been able to recognize that these fuzzy feelings were really based on what I held dearest in my heart—my deepest values and yearnings. On the journey home, you will begin to recognize and embody your innermost values. These are your core beliefs, assumptions, or barometers of meaning that, when you are listening, may guide you and give meaning and purpose to your life. For most of us, these have never been articulated, have been forgotten, or have been beaten out of us by family or culture. As we return to our core values, we return to what we hold most dear. Confidence in our own potential and goodness emerges. As you come home to your own values, you come home to the desires of your heart. This is one of the most remarkable effects of regular meditation practice, and one that is often overlooked. We often think of meditation as an escape, but many students I have worked with report of its powerful ability to return us to our true purpose and to a life of authenticity. One step at a time, you begin to live life from your *courageous self.*

Coming Home from a World of Conflicting Messages

I grew up confused. There were so many choices, so many paths, and so many conflicting messages. I received one set of messages from my family, another set of messages from religious communities, another set from friends and peers, and many others from the culture at large. The modern world gives us *all* very conflicting messages. We are told that we should think for ourselves and that we should have intellectual autonomy, and are also told what we should believe. We are told that we are inherently worthy, and are also told that we are only as good as what we produce and consume. We are taught that all persons have rights, but also that some groups are more worthy than others. We are told that happiness begins with the heart, but also that happiness results from material success and possessions. We are taught that success is a result of hard work, effort, and skill, but are also told that success is determined by status and whom we know. We are told that everything is fine and rosy, and also that the world is being destroyed before our very eyes. What is true and who do we believe? Coming home is about coming home to your own strength and intuition and quieting the conflicting external voices. On the journey home, you *will* come home to your own inner confidence. You will be able to sort through all of this and forge a path that is unique to yourself with confidence and clarity.

Coming Home from Too Much Information

Most of us are living in a constant state of information overload. This is the most common stressor that people report in meditation classes. In one given day, I may take in more information than some of my ancestors did during their entire lives! Multiple information streams bombard us at practically all times. Think about the past few hours of your life or about a typical day. What sorts and types of information have you been taking in? Through habit or necessity, the bombardment is nonstop and the assault, for most of us, continues to increase. Our brains become overwhelmed and anxiety results. This causes many problems. For one, it is simply too much to handle; We become overwhelmed. I get overwhelmed often. How about you? I now, however, am better equipped to recognize that this is occurring and to take proactive steps to manage this. Through the perspective of *Wholesome Mindfulness,* you will be able to do this as well.

Coming Home to Who You Are: You Are Not What You Buy!

Each of us has lived our entire life in the Age of the Marketplace. Advertisers, and their clever pitches for our attention and dollars, want us to think that our very existence is at stake. I remember thinking that I would literally die if my mom would not buy me the Woody the Woodpecker cereal bowl that I kept seeing advertised on morning cartoons. They want us to think that we have to possess their goods or services in order for us to be the person we want to be. Advertisers want to cultivate in us a *need* for their particular product and to have our self-perceived identity forged with the given product. For example, I feel so much more sophisticated and refined in my Patagonia jacket!

I bet we all can identify certain products or brands as positive indicators of status and others as less so. For example, I notice a tendency in myself to evaluate the character of others by the brands of the clothes they are wearing or automobiles they are driving. In the process of coming home through the practices of *Wholesome Mindfulness,* you will discover a level of identity much deeper and more authentic than the identity you have been indoctrinated into via marketing and products.

Coming Home from Excessive Busyness

For most of us, we are always doing. A teacher of mine refers to this as a "do-istic" culture. When not *doing* to produce, we are *doing* to entertain and distract. *Be busy at all costs* is one of the underlying mantras of modern culture. Busyness is not inherently bad. In fact, it is necessary to function and survive. Who among us has not felt a sense of satisfaction having completed a successful project? Being busy in the service of a desired goal, for me at least, is an important component of a meaningful life. But being busy has transformed from something to engage in voluntarily and willfully in order to produce a particular outcome to a compulsion. Many of us have lost the ability to relax, at least in healthy ways, and many students I have worked with report feeling anxious or inadequate when "not doing." At a core emotional level, we are indoctrinated to feel that we must remain busy at all costs. As a result, introspection, self-awareness, and inner contentment have been sacrificed. Coming home through *Wholesome Mindfulness* involves waking up from this compulsion and reconnecting with inner contentment.

Coming Home to Shared Humanity

We evolved via a tribal mindset, but this mindset is outdated. Unconsciously at least, we have a tendency to break the world into good tribes and bad tribes. Our consciousness involves a built-in appraisal system. Basically, when we become aware of something, we evaluate whether it is important to our own self-interest, and if so, how it will impact us. This appraisal process occurs on the spot and is largely outside of our awareness and control. Much of our evaluations involve evaluations of others, and this is very important. But we get ourselves in trouble when we do this unconsciously and automatically. This results in stereotypes and biases. Fortunately, we are at a place where many people want a better world. I sure do, and I imagine that you do, too. Our old ways of collecting into groups are outdated and many of us want a new way to live in community. Meditation practice, and the practices offered in *Wholesome Mindfulness,* afford you the opportunity to become part of this new and emerging mindset, a mindset of shared humanity. Such a mindset will make your life more meaningful and will help foster an optimistic vision of our collective future.

When teaching, I often say that we are constantly *putting others into boxes, and these boxes determine how we respond to them emotionally.* One person's suffering might elicit a compassionate response. Another person's suffering might not, all depending on how I have sized them up. It is time to evolve past the tribal mindset. The good news is that we have tools to do so, and research is showing that they are effective. In an increasingly interconnected world, overcoming the tribal mindset is literally necessary for our survival. Moreover, it feels healthy and authentic and leads to a more meaningful life. It is amazing that we can alter these implicit and unconscious assumptions that we have about others. On a perceptual level, we can train our minds to perceive the shared humanity in everyone. Rather than noticing and focusing on differences first, we can actually train ourselves to see the commonalities we share at a very automatic and instinctual level. On the journey home, you will learn to tap increasingly into this attitude of shared humanity, and thus, to have more connection to others and less reactivity.

Coming Home to Your Place in the World

Coming home is not only an internal process. It also may involve tapping into a calling, a sense of purpose in this messy world. For much of my life I felt a little out of sorts, and that I really did not fit anywhere. This is a sentiment that I often hear from my meditation students in one form or another. As the pace of life accelerates, and we become increasingly saturated with technology and devices, a sense of unease also often increases. Paradoxically, we modern humans are both connected and isolated from others in unprecedented ways. With the touch of a finger or the click of a mouse, I have the opportunity for instantaneous connection with almost anyone that I have ever known. Through social media platforms, I have been reunited with countless friends, and have been able to forge meaningful new relationships with many others. This is fabulous! And yet, there is often a shallowness and lack of intimacy to these connections, and they are no substitute for true human connections. The more that our relationships are primarily based on technology, the less satisfying these relationships can become and the more that loneliness increases. Do you ever feel disconnected or lonely after spending too much time on social media? The practices of *Wholesome Mindfulness* can afford you the opportunity to reclaim—or to find—your place in the world. Coming home to your heart is also coming home to your calling, coming home to your niche.

Coming Home to Emotional Nourishment

For the past several years I have been working explicitly with emotions. Though I have been meditating and working in mental health for many years, it is only until fairly recently that I have fully realized the importance of this work. During the opening session of a training retreat for teachers of *Mindfulness-Based Emotional Balance*, during introductions I said, "I come from a long line of people with no clue about emotions." I have a fairly sharp wit, and this was intended to be funny and witty. And it got a good laugh. But in working with my own emotions and assisting others in their own work,

I have come to realize that most of us have very little real insight into emotions.

From my own experience and from the testimonies of students, I have come to see that many, if not most, modern people do not really know what emotions are or how to work with them skillfully. To a large extent, our lives are guided by our emotions. We may be aware of strong emotional surges, or that some emotional experiences are desirable and others undesirable, but that might be about it. Coming home involves coming home to our emotional reality. A perspective of *Wholesome Mindfulness* will allow you to be able to non-judgmentally recognize your emotions and to have more choices available to you in how to respond to them. You will become more emotionally literate and more able to provide emotional nourishment to yourself and others. The overall result will be a more emotionally balanced and meaningful life.

Coming Home from Self-Sabotage

Often, we get in our own way. We may even sabotage our own trajectory toward health and wholeness. Have you ever wanted something very badly, and then gotten in your own way of achieving this? Have you ever done things that run counter to your core values? Do you ever wonder why you don't follow through with your own dreams and aspirations? I can unequivocally answer yes to each of these questions, as can many of my students. We have many competing desires and motivations, and sometimes—maybe even most of the time—the ones that do not represent our true and authentic values and intentions predominate. We are often our own worst enemies. Coming home involves tapping into our core values and being able to act from them. You will be better able to be a friend and ally to yourself. With a mindset of *Wholesome Mindfulness*, you can even become your own best friend.

Beginning the Journey

You are already on a journey home. The practices and perspective of *Wholesome Mindfulness* will help you to clearly articulate your journey and to pursue it with conscious awareness. It will help you to take the lead in your own life, and to lead from the heart. All that is needed for this journey is you. You already have all of the necessary supplies for the journey home. You have the necessary tools. These tools may need to be enhanced or refined, and you may need to train yourself on how to use them properly, but you have the tools and are ready to embark. Give yourself a message of appreciation for being at this stage. Give yourself a message of appreciation for having the courage to embark on this journey. Give yourself a message of appreciation for following your heart. Give yourself a message of appreciation for cultivating and following your *courageous self.*

Introductory Self-Reflective Activity: Why Am I here?

Now, I invite you to gently begin the journey home. As indicated, the formal practices of *Wholesome Mindfulness* will be introduced in Chapter 4. But for any endeavor, it is important to have a sense of motivation from the get-go. This short exercise will help you to tap into a sense of motivation and purpose as you begin your journey. Think of it as a compass that you take with you on your way, always there for you to help you to stay on course.

Much will be said about this later, but one key to working with reflective practices is *not* to expect anything in particular. Just do the reflective exercise and see what happens. Sometimes just asking questions like this opens doors, even if no answers emerge, because it is a pathway to new ways of self-relating. So now I invite you to get your journal or a piece of paper and to engage in the following self-reflective activity.

Breathe, relax, and gently and mindfully write down your responses to the following three questions. Make your responses as short or as long as you would like.

What motivated me to want to read this book?

Why am I drawn to mindfulness and meditation?

What parts of my life do I cherish the most?

Now close your eyes for a minute or two and simply breathe.

Feel your body breathing and allow your reflections to settle into your mind.

Please note that all self-reflective activities, guided meditations, and embodied exercises in the book, along with bonus activities, are accessible at the book's resource page: www.dentgitchel.com/pursuingpurpose.

Chapter 2

The Path of My Journey Home

It was a beautiful sunny day in the summer of 1990. I was coming to meet my faculty advisor for the first time at Hendrix College, a small liberal arts college not far from Little Rock, Arkansas, where I had grown up. I was returning to college after a three-and-a-half-year "sabbatical," after being unable to complete my studies at a previous institution.

During this absence from school, I came to question everything I had ever been taught about myself or the world around me. Looking back, I was alone in the world and really was unsure where to look for guidance. I was searching for something, not even aware of what it was that I was looking for.

This path had involved various odd jobs, a basically itinerant lifestyle, a love for the music and culture of the Grateful Dead, reading many books (primarily spiritual and self-help oriented), and many travels and adventures. And though I could not articulate it during this time, I was developing an affinity for Eastern spirituality. Pretty much everything that I knew, or thought I knew, about reality was shattered during my time away from school. But what was left was not nothing. Something else was emerging.

For reasons that I am still unsure of, I decided to declare myself as a double major in physics and philosophy. And for reasons that I am equally unsure of, this advisor whom I had never met before suggested that I take a course being offered in Buddhism, a course that altered the trajectory of my life.

In my philosophy classes, I found a sense of open inquiry and reflective thinking that I had never before experienced. I felt nourished on many levels. I felt validated, accepted, and listened to. I was able to thrive in an environment where free thinking was encouraged and modeled. I was able to come to the table with all of the hard problems that I had grappled with, to articulate my questions in a coherent way, and to have these questions respected and heard. Moreover, through the study of the formal history of Western and Eastern thought, I became aware that these questions had been around for millennia, and that many of the greatest minds that have ever lived have grappled with such deep questions.

In some ways, my previous three years' experiences had provided a strong backdrop to the formal philosophy that I was now studying and helped me to be open to new ideas. I had seen a lot, experienced a lot, and become part of a community much larger than myself during this time and was open to exploring possibilities.

Though I did not really know it, I was a spiritual seeker at heart. I embarked on risky journeys and encountered important life lessons along the way. I experienced love and kindness from strangers that to this day gives me hope in the human condition. I experienced highs and lows of experience beyond my imagination, and these have remained as my barometers of human capacities and possibilities. I developed a strong faith in the human heart and great appreciation for the frailty of human life, a strong disdain for those who say that they have the answer, and a strong belief that spirituality should embrace the messiness of life and should be applicable to the actual spaces in which we live.

If the study of philosophy, in general, provided the fuel, then the class on Buddhism provided the rocket ship for the launch that has powered the trajectory of my life. This journey has taken me to various places, including work in mental health and academia, and the study of "mainstream" psychological and counseling perspectives. But the journey has always been rooted in the training that I received in college about varieties of religious and philosophical perspectives, coupled with my own experiences outside of mainstream culture. I have always been fueled by the underlying urge to "figure shit out," and this naturally and eventually involved figuring out my own mind. And this, my friend, is an ongoing process.

The good news I discovered in Buddhism is basically that there is more to the story than the suffering that encompasses our lives. This suffering is real, but it is not the end of the story. It is not the end of the story because this suffering has causes, and these causes can be examined and eliminated. The good news is that we can do something about this human predicament. Moreover, not only can we do something, but there is a well-established path laid out for us. There are proven methods, techniques, and guides to help us on this path.

In my undergraduate encounter with Buddhism, I also engaged in the simple and traditional meditation technique of "following the breath" that I continue to use each day and that is shared with you here in Chapter 4.

The consistent driving force in my life over the past three decades has been to study my own mind and life as much as possible through formal and informal contemplative practices and to try and engage in the world in ways that are authentic. After my initial introduction to Buddhism, I devoured every book I could find on the topic for many years, while also continuing to pursue the practice of meditation.

And this was the world before the Internet. I would travel to try and find new bookstores to visit, and increasingly became interested in Tibetan Buddhism. The first time I read a book by His Holiness the Dalai Lama, a prominent contemporary leader of Tibetan Buddhism, I felt that I was being called home.

My path home has been fueled by curiosity and confidence, but I have also encountered a lot of confusion, insecurity, and self-doubt. I was beset by many questions: There are so many practices and paths, how do I find a path for me? There are so many different types of Buddhism, but are they even the same religion? Can I study Buddhist practices and not be a Buddhist? Are rituals and exotic cultural practices necessary? How do I find personal guidance to proceed on the contemplative path? Is it alright to adapt practices on my own? And importantly, how do I integrate contemplative practices from a foreign tradition into my own modern world? Currently, these types of questions have moved to the forefront of public discussions about the interface of Buddhism and modernity. To me, they have been my guiding personal questions.

Fortunately, that initial foundation of meditation instruction that I received during my first encounter with Buddhism stayed with me. Though I would stray from time to time, and take many productive and unproductive side trips, I would return time and time again to the basic practice of meditation on the breath. And yet, part of me was never quite sure in the early years if I was doing it right. This was often unacknowledged and under the surface, but it was always there and was clear as day. Part of me felt that I was making progress and truly digesting profound and authentic teachings, and part of me felt very unsure. What I needed was a guide to clarify things, point me in the right direction, and say, "You got this." I hope that this book can serve as that resource for you.

Gradually, my meditation practice became steadier and I developed relationships with teachers and specific traditions. As such, my own sense of authenticity increased. A turning point for me was becoming a formal student of compassion meditation practices of Tibetan Buddhism. These practices are deep, profound, and practically oriented. I had explored some of these practices on my own for some years and had read many books, but they had not completely stuck. Even so, I was a firm believer. They had given me some sustenance and courage, helping me to sit with my dying grandparents and with my professional work providing services to individuals with serious and persistent mental illnesses. Yet many questions remained: Do I need to believe in the underlying worldview to engage in these practices? Is it safe to offer these potentially healing practices to others? Under the guidance of traditional Tibetan teachers, I was able to tie together a lot of loose ends and to develop confidence. In the years since, I have had the opportunity to study with a variety of teachers and to be engaged in the development and delivery of secular-based approaches to meditation.

Gradually, I began to teach meditation techniques and mindsets to others. At first, I did this informally with clients or friends who expressed interest. I then became certified as a teacher of *Compassion Cultivation Training,* a program developed at the Center for Compassion and Altruism Research and Education at Stanford University. It is an eight-week training program that is primarily a secular adaptation of some of the compassion practices associated with Tibetan Buddhism. I have also participated in the teacher training program for *Mindfulness Based Emotional Balance* and have received instruction and training on how to teach others from my Buddhist teachers.

Much of my training has been in terms of Buddhist meditation and practice, and Buddhist theory and practices are the foundation of the orientation and of many of the contemplative practices presented here. But this is not a book on Buddhism. *Wholesome Mindfulness* is based largely on my experiences practicing and teaching, on how to engage effectively with modern life using contemplative practices. It is a friendly guide to help you on your own path, whatever it might be, from my heart to yours. And, having worked with hundreds of others, it is advice that I think is timely and will be beneficial. *Wholesome Mindfulness* is an approach to contemplative practices geared for the modern mind.

We can all learn to walk the path of mindfulness and courage, but we must take one step at a time. With each step, your confidence and insight into your own purpose and capacities will increase and you will be better able to live an authentic and meaningful life. You will begin to come home to who you really are.

The Transformative Changes Ahead

It is quite important to have some strategies available for navigating such a journey and to know of some of the obstacles and challenges that might be encountered on the way to the destination. In our case, the destination in hand is some sort of *change* in experience. Typically, there is some sort of perceived dissatisfaction that propels us to engage in contemplative practices. How about you? What is it that motivates you to pursue meditation strategies involving mindfulness and compassion? For me, it was certainly some sort of sense that *life is not quite right* and that meditation practices might offer a solution to this situation.

Now, I would like to point out some of the factors contributing to the occurrence of transformative change when we engage in the practices of *Wholesome Mindfulness* or other contemplative practices. In other words, what is going on? What is happening to us as we practice that makes the contemplative path both challenging and rewarding? Why is meditation helpful and how can its effects be maximized? These insights are gleaned both from research and from my own experiences, both with myself and from helping others.

Confidence: You Can Do This!

Confidence is an important part of any endeavor. The more we develop confidence, the better chance we will succeed.

Think of learning a new skill or engaging in a time-consuming project. To be successful, it is necessary to have confidence in both your abilities and that you have the resources that you need. In short, you must feel that you *can* do what is required and that you have what you *need.* I am hoping to help you have the confidence that you *can* meditate and that you have what you need.

One of the biggest barriers of beginning (and experienced) meditators is a lack of confidence. I have experienced this in my own life and have heard this from countless students. It is normal, not pathological, but needs to be acknowledged and worked through. It is important to recognize that confidence can be trained by taking very small steps. If you lack confidence, there is nothing wrong with you. You just need to put one foot in front of the other and confidence will gently and gradually develop, until it becomes strong and stable and serves as the foundation of all that you do.

It is quite natural for the brain to fluctuate between extremes of greater and lesser confidence. Having small accomplishments and successes along your path largely builds confidence. Each time you have a small success, a message is sent to your brain: *I can do this.* As more and more successes are experienced, you begin to agree, and uncontrived confidence emerges. This unshakable confidence will underlie all that you do. Yes, you can do this! Or rather, you *will* do this!

Believing in the Result

To accomplish anything, you must first feel that it is worth accomplishing. Psychologists sometimes refer to this as an *outcome expectation.* This refers to what we think will happen—or what is at stake—upon successful completion. Ultimately, it comes down to the question, *does this matter?* Thus, we assess not only whether we *can* do something, but also whether we *should* do something. What is the payoff? What is at stake? The brain is a prediction machine. As you proceed on your path, your conviction will grow, based on your own experiences, that what you are doing really matters. And, I am here to assure you that this is true. Your path matters. Do not let your self-doubt, or anyone else, tell you otherwise. As you experience results, your confidence and your practice will naturally become stronger. In my case, as I began to see benefits from meditation emerge into daily life, my confidence increased and my practice became stronger.

Retraining the Mind and Brain

In practicing *Wholesome Mindfulness*, you are largely training your mind to experience yourself and the world differently. How we experience the world is largely a matter of deeply ingrained habits. How we experience ourselves is likewise largely a matter of deeply ingrained habits. We typically think of habits in terms of physical behaviors. But here, an important point is being made that our actual experiences are largely a result of habituation. In the field of neuroscience, there is a popular phrase: *neurons that fire together wire together*. Our brains are made up of countless millions of neurons, and these neurons are connected through countless webs of interconnecting pathways. Each time we have an experience, the brain is stimulated in a particular way, and neurons fire in particular patterns. In meditation training, the brain is gradually and systematically being trained to operate differently. When you engage with the contemplative path, you are literally rewiring the hardware underlying your experiences. Think of the practices of *Wholesome Mindfulness* as healthy exercises for the brain.

Neuroscientists label this capacity to change our own hardwiring as *neuroplasticity*. This concept is quite revolutionary. The brain is constantly changing. Though we become hardwired to experience the world (and ourselves) in particular ways, this wiring is not static, but is changing throughout our lives. Our brains are plastic and malleable, and there is a feedback loop between the brain and the human experience. To a large extent, the way your brain is wired influences all of your experiences, but the causality is not exclusively one-way. Our experiences, too, influence brain functioning. By developing new mental habits, you are actually developing a new brain. By engaging in the practices and perspectives of *Wholesome Mindfulness*, you are installing a new "operating system" —one that is healthier and more authentic to who you really are.

Befriending Ourselves

Are you a friend to yourself? I have to honestly say that many times I am not a friend to myself. Most of my life I have been my own worst critic and have sabotaged many a worthwhile endeavor. For many of us, the default attitude to ourselves is not one of kindness. Rather, we are typically stern and critical. For most modern people, like you and me, a critical component of psychological growth is the gradual transformation of our relationship to ourselves from one of criticism and harshness to one of support and friendliness. How does a good friend treat you? Can you imagine treating yourself as a good friend would? For many years I could not imagine this. In the practice of *Wholesome Mindfulness*, you will gradually learn to be a friend to yourself. This is one of the biggest benefits of meditation practice and one of the most common goals of meditation students. People often come to meditation classes because of a self-identified need to be friendly toward themselves, or at the very least, an acknowledgment of how hard they typically are on themselves.

There is a relatively new breed of contemplative practices falling under the umbrella of *self-compassion*. Such practices allow for a radical transformation of the ways we relate to ourselves. I became formally introduced to this type of mindset during my training to become a teacher of Stanford's *Compassion Cultivation Training* program. Looking back, I am aware of a strong resistance I had to this approach. I resisted doing the practices and saw myself as above this type of approach. After all, I had been studying "authentic" meditation for many years. What did this kind of stuff have to offer me after all? It is for sissies!

Boy was I wrong. I noticed some of my respected colleagues courageously engaging in self-reflection in response to the self-compassion practices and struggling with self-criticism, self-doubt, and self-hatred in their own practices. This was a very eye-opening moment for me. I made a vow to myself at that very moment to reapproach this material, and I have been working with self-compassion practices regularly since then. They have transformed my relationship with myself and have given me a new perspective on traditional mindfulness and compassion practices. In some ways, self-compassion now underlies all of my personal practices as well as all of my teaching. As you engage in the contemplative path of *Wholesome Mindfulness*, you can expect for your *attitude* toward yourself to gradually be transformed to one of support and friendliness. You can love and support yourself just as a trusted friend would.

Learning to Evaluate Yourself, Others, and the World Differently

As a biological creature, much of what you do is to evaluate your surroundings. For basic survival, it has been constantly necessary to be vigilant and on guard. Part of our biological heritage has been this instinct to be in a constant appraisal process. We are constantly asking ourselves: *Does this matter? And, if so, what is at stake?* We are doing this all of the time, typically below the surface of conscious awareness. By the time that something comes into conscious awareness, these questions have already been addressed and answered. Much of this appraisal is done from the perspective of the *cowardly self.* From no fault of our own, we have been conditioned to view the world through the lenses of fear and self-preservation. The result of this is a highly *reactionary* state of mind. One of the most profound effects of contemplative practice can be on our automatic evaluations. Through the practices and perspectives of *Wholesome Mindfulness,* you will be able to gradually *develop the capacity to choose rather than react.* As a result, you will have more ability to choose to be the person that you truly want to be.

The Lenses of Experience

We are often blind to what is truly going on. We may think of ourselves as objective and rational, but in reality, we are often experiencing reality through the lenses of our own biases and projections. The mind is like a film projector. Often what we see is only a version of the truth, a version corresponding to the projectors of our minds. When teaching, I often refer to this as the *lenses of experience*. Experience is not pure. Rather, it is filtered through our own lenses. And we are very adaptable. We have many different sets of glasses that we can put on. And very few of them are rose-colored! They come in many styles, colors, and fashions, but one thing they all have in common is that they filter our experience of reality. Moreover, we typically are not aware that we are seeing the world through a particular lens.

This is possibly most readily observable in the context of strong emotions. Think of a time when you got very angry. How did you perceive things while in this state of anger? Did it skew your perception of reality? Were you motivated to act on this anger? Did you actually act on this anger? Anger, and other strong emotions, blind us to thinking clearly. When I am angry, I see things through the logic of anger. The anger has its own logic, and experience is filtered in support of that logic. And importantly, we typically are not even aware even that we are wearing this lens until we are out from under its spell. We literally wake up to our anger, or perhaps to some actions that we have done because of it. *Wholesome Mindfulness* encourages noticing the lenses we wear and having more choices in how to respond to what we see through their influence. As you practice, your ability to do this will increase and you will develop more emotional balance and flexibility.

Reformulating Meditation

Sometimes, we approach meditation practice as one more thing to knock off of our to-do list. And, in the context of the busyness of modern life, it must be approached this way at times. I know for me I have to make time for daily meditation practice, and to strategize about how to effectively fit it into an already-busy schedule. A wholesome approach to meditation, however, is to approach it as something that is integrated into all aspects of life. From this perspective, what happens *on the cushion* is not an escape, but rather, is tied to all that we do *off the cushion*. The ultimate aim of contemplative practices, according to the *Wholesome Mindfulness* approach presented here, is to help us to lead wholesome lives in *all* aspects of life. As such, we are training ourselves in a mindset, an attitude, and a set of skills, which can be taken out into the world and used in all life situations. By taking one small step after another, we are gradually and gently learning to be in the world in a new and more authentic way. Sometimes this will feel quite natural and sometimes it may feel contrived, but it is important to remember that if we consistently engage in the practice, things are shifting under the surface. Our experience is being gradually transformed. *Wholesome Mindfulness* is about coming home to a more authentic life. Let us continue the journey of coming home.

Chapter 3

Cultivating the Right Attitude of Meditation

How we work with *Wholesome Mindfulness* practices—or any contemplative techniques—is crucial. There is a tendency to focus on *what* we are doing and not so much on *how* we are doing it. This is particularly true in meditation. We are used to doing, and construct much of our identity on what we *do* (or feel that we *should* be doing). Any focus on the *how* typically emphasizes *technique.* In the context of meditation, I might ask myself, *What should I be doing in order to meditate correctly?* This is a typical way of approaching practice: *How should I be sitting? On what should I focus my attention?*

It is certainly important to know techniques, and plenty will be offered in this book. But this focus on doing, in my opinion, can miss a lot. What is missing here is an examination of what

I call the *attitude of meditation*. In many ways, our attitude can make or break our progress.

My first exposure to meditation was *zazen*, a mindfulness-based practice from the Zen Buddhist tradition. I had been introduced to some of the philosophical foundations of Buddhism with which I strongly resonated and was at least partially aware of a large amount of discomfort, discontent, and suffering in my life. I saw meditation as an answer, as a way of embodying the philosophy that I was drawn to and alleviating my suffering. So, I dove in.

I am forever grateful that I was able to learn "authentic" meditation with my first exposure. My college professor had an established daily meditation practice and an authentic "Zen Master," Roshi Fukushima, visited our class from Japan. The two had forged a close relationship years before and he had been visiting the college annually for some years. We learned the formal practice of meditation during class, and I also participated in a weekend-long retreat offered to the greater community. As I remember, great emphasis was given to the postural aspects of sitting meditation, followed by directions to follow the breath as we inhaled and exhaled. We were instructed to "simply" follow each cycle of breath, and when the mind wandered, to bring it back to the breathing process. Counting the breaths was offered as a foundational technique to help keep the mind from straying too much. Silently recite "one" on the exhalation, then "two" and so on until "ten" was reached, and then come back to "one" and begin again.

We meditated for about 20 minutes in our first exposure to meditation. I was so excited and ready. Roshi has such a strong and noble presence, combined with a strong dose of humor. I wanted some of that! Much to my surprise, however, what I primarily noticed was a bunch of pain and a very hyperactive mind. I was bombarded by thoughts: *Damn, I can't do this! There is something wrong with me! This is intolerable!* I was not yet at a stage to articulate, or even to understand, that I am not my thoughts and the messages that they give me do not have to be listened to or followed. And so began a 30-year process of gradually learning to watch my mind and become less captive to it.

But the self-criticism was not the only voice. Though the voice that said *you can't do this* was definitely there, and still is to some degree, this was not the only voice. There was also a softer and gentler voice, perhaps more vague and fuzzy, telling me *you can do this.* To this day, if I listen, it is there—a distant call beckoning me home. It is sometimes drowned out by the noises of hyperactivity and self-criticism. But in times of silence, it is there. It is a trusted friend and never leaves. *Come Home! You. Can. Do. This.* It is there for me. It is there for you. It is a call to come home to your path, whatever that might be. The journey never ends, and in many ways, the path is the journey, but it is the most meaningful journey you will ever take.

What I needed on my journey was a gentle hand to guide me. They were probably around, but I was blind to them. I am offering mine to you. You do not have to do this alone. The road home is yours and yours alone, but gentle and compassionate guides are very helpful. To that end, I now offer some strategies for working with meditation practices.

Cultivate the Attitude of a Scientist

One of my teachers sometimes says, “Be a scientist in the laboratory of your own life.” The first time I heard this statement it captivated me, and I use it consistently both in my own practice and in teaching others. Like so many other instructions about how to engage in contemplative practices, it is simple, but yet difficult, to put into practice. However, I firmly believe this statement is pointing us toward an important facet of how we should approach meditation practices, whether we are beginners or are more advanced. From this perspective, what would it mean to approach our own life? Basically, this is asking us to be open and inquisitive about our own experiences.

The mind of a scientist is one of *curiosity* and *open inquiry*. We may think of a scientist as a technician; as a person in a laboratory, or as a manufacturer of technology. But the true mind of a scientist is open to possibilities and curious. Think of something in your life that you have been truly curious about. The curious mind is open, engaged, and tinged with a bit of excitement. The outcome is unknown, which is part of the excitement. We simply do not know what the outcome of our investigations will be. In the context of contemplative practices, we adopt this mindset to our own lives and our own experiences. We become our own case studies, which is very difficult to do. This is the mind I invite you to bring to your practice of *Wholesome Mindfulness*.

Typically, we investigate our own lives through a lens of judgment and expectation. I can get caught up in expectations about how my experience *should* be, which leads to feelings of frustration and self-criticism when I do not meet these expectations. Thankfully, though, meditation practice can give you a little space to loosen up a bit and simply be with what is occurring with curiosity rather than constantly evaluating. For most of us, we have lost the ability to approach our own lives with an attitude of curiosity. We have had this beaten out of us by family, educational institutions, and the larger culture. To have an attitude of a scientist is to be curious about yourself. Think of something that you have legitimate curiosity about. Recognize what this feels like. Now, imagine bringing this attitude with you as you begin meditation practice.

A scientific mindset also involves objectivity. This type of objectivity involves the courageous ability to look the truth in the eye, to see what arises as it truly is and not what we hope for it to be. It is courageous—particularly in the case of our own lives and experiences—because we have to set aside our expectations, desires, and prejudices, and be honest with whatever occurs. Moreover, we have been trained almost exclusively to seek truth outside of ourselves, and this external focus has made most of us illiterate to our own experiences. To be objective in the context presented here is to be objective with our own lives and experiences. This. Is. Hard. But it is very important to recognize this at the beginning. It is hard but it is *hard for us all.* You are reading these words, so you are ripe for this type of inquiry. You are ripe for meditation and the practices of *Wholesome Mindfulness.* I congratulate you on your courage and the transformations in your life that such courage will bring.

Approach your own life and experiences with curiosity and objectivity and see what is working for you and how. Be a scientist in the laboratory of your own life.

Integrate Practice into Daily Life

We often think of meditation as something that is done formally, in a meditation session, and it is. But that is not all it is. Ultimately, it is a self-reflective awareness that can be taken into all walks of life. Indeed, to some degree, this is the ultimate point. If it does not help you to live your life more effectively, then what good is it? It is not simply a mini vacation, a retreat from busy life activities. If that were it, then it would be no different than taking a break to watch a movie.

Ultimately, it becomes about *engaging more authentically with life rather than retreating from life.* We learn to do this little by little, by taking baby steps.

In this book you will be presented with various "embodied practices." These are short and very doable practices that are easily integrated into daily life. *I cannot emphasize strongly enough how important this is.* They appear very simple and can easily be undervalued or overlooked. However, I highly encourage you to integrate these into your daily life. They are important for several reasons. They are easy and will provide you with a level of momentum that can be very helpful. Remember that in engaging with contemplative practices, we are in effect retraining ourselves to think, experience, and act differently. These "small" practices greatly facilitate this. They reinforce formal meditation practices and help to integrate the benefits into daily life, and in turn, they help to improve the quality of formal contemplative practices. Formal and informal practices feed off of one another, resulting ultimately in a more integrative and contemplative approach to living life as a whole. These brief embodied practices are a very important part of creating a perspective of *Wholesome Mindfulness.*

Cultivating a Gentle Mindset

Be gentle with yourself. If you only take one piece of advice to heart, make it this! Be disciplined, focused, and goal-oriented, but stay gentle. Our attitude toward life, and to ourselves, is often rigid and tight. Whether consciously or not, the default mode of operation for most of us in the modern world is very serious, particularly in areas of life that are important to us. Here, you are encouraged to adopt a very gentle mindset to your own experiences and your own trajectory of growth. And again, this will likely be a new habit for you. We typically drive ourselves very hard, or else drop our effort completely because we feel that we are *not good enough*. Do you resonate with this? This is a common sentiment reported by students that I work with. You are encouraged here to develop gentleness with yourself that may be quite new. It may even be new enough that it makes no sense to you. That was the case for me. I may have appeared to others as laid-back and carefree, but internally, that was not the case at all. I was wound up tight. Though it might have been outside of my conscious awareness, I was pushing myself and beating myself up all the time. And, in my experiences, this is a malady—a mindset—that is extremely prevalent in our modern world. In this book, you will be nudged again and again to cultivate a gentle attitude toward your own life.

An Attitude of Self-Kindness

This is akin to the above attitude of gentleness but more personal. I encourage you to adopt a spirit of kindness to yourself that you might have toward a favorite friend or relative. Take a few moments and allow your mind to settle. Just breathe in and out and notice your body breathing. Now bring to mind a person (or animal) that naturally brings a smile to your face, someone that you instinctively care for. As you are calmly breathing, just keep this person in mind or imagine they are there in front of you. You might even remember a positive memory of being with them. Hold this thought or memory in mind as you continue to breathe. Now, place one or both hands in the center of your chest. Feel your chest gently rise and fall with the rhythm of the breathing. How do you feel? Spacious? Warm? Open? Relaxed? Whatever it is, take note of it. I suspect it is very different from how you typically feel as you relate to yourself and your own experiences.

In this book, you will be encouraged to take this attitude of kindness and friendliness and apply it to meditation and self-reflective practices. This is probably something you are not used to, and you will be reminded again and again to adopt this attitude of self-kindness. As my own testimonial shows, this attitude is not one that I cultivated for many years. Though my intentions were good, and I wanted the best for myself, I was in some ways treating myself as the enemy. And this is not uncommon, even for experienced meditators. It is quite possible to progress in the areas of focus and concentration and other "exalted states" but to do so with an underlying attitude of self-hatred or self-criticism. This is counterproductive on many levels. *You are encouraged here to be a friend to yourself.* It takes time and it may always be a work in progress, but it can help your life to be meaningful in many ways. Self-kindness will help every aspect of your life and is an important component in the development of *Wholesome Mindfulness.*

Be Patient and Allow the Results to Emerge

In the modern world, we often look for immediate results. This is evident in every aspect of our culture. We jump from diet to diet or from one self-improvement project to another. When we don't see immediate results, we go on to the next project, relationship, or whatever. I have been guilty of this thousands of times; how about you? This attitude is counterproductive in many areas of our lives, but particularly in the cultivation of *Wholesome Mindfulness.* An effect refers, basically, to the immediate experience of a given practice—what effect the practice has in the moment or immediately afterward. Results are what emerge over time as a result of our practices. It becomes problematic when we evaluate our practices—and our progress—in terms of effects rather than results. This mistake is very common, and I cannot highlight it enough, particularly with respect to the earlier advice to *be a scientist in the laboratory of your own life.* The advice here is to be gentle, to develop a doable commitment, and to give yourself time to evaluate the results objectively. You will notice the results of a regular meditation practice, but these results may be subtle and emerge gradually over time. The benefits are often occurring below the surface, and will emerge in ways that you might not expect.

With an attitude of gentleness and self-compassion, your life *will* be transformed; it just might not be evident *every* time you sit down to practice or engage in a self-reflective activity.

Buddhist author Ken McLeod presents the distinction between immediate effects and results in terms of an example of exercise. Perhaps I want to improve my physical fitness and become in better shape. I might then establish an overall goal of doing so. I might then adopt a regimen of practices, say jogging, to achieve this end. I devise a plan and then begin to jog, perhaps working my way up to a desired speed and distance. Along the way, I will encounter many effects. Some days I may be sore and tired. Some days I might be energetic. Some days might be relatively easy, while others are a complete struggle. If I evaluate my progress based on the effects of any given practice session, my interpretation will likely be mistaken. On a bad day, I am likely to judge my progress negatively and may even become disillusioned and even quit my program. On a good day, I am likely to judge my progress overly optimistically, perhaps leading to unrealistic expectations that will lead to future disillusionment.

However, if I assess my progress over time based on results that emerge, my conclusions are likely to be much more valid. This is very important because people are often taught to let go of expectations when engaging in meditation practices and sometimes confusion emerges around this. Foregoing expectation does not mean not to have hope or to have a desire for progress, however that is defined for you. What would be the point of that? Typically, but not always, we are drawn to meditation because of some sort of discontent in our lives that we would like to have lessened. That is healthy and natural, and it is important to evaluate whether our practices are actually working toward that end. We are making a mistake, however, when we do this based on the effects of any given day or practice session. Sharon Salzberg, a prominent meditation teacher and cofounder of the Insight Meditation Society, recommends practicing for 15 minutes a day for 28 days and then evaluating your practice; this is very sound advice. That is enough time to see results, but a short enough time for a realistic commitment.

If you practice regularly, you will have many ups and downs in your practice. That is natural and par for the course. Think of any long or sustained project that you have been involved in. Isn't this the case? It takes a level of perseverance and determination. Understanding this distinction between effects and results can be an important factor in developing and maintaining such perseverance. We can then use the mind of a scientist and evaluate and assess our contemplative path. Here, I suggest to you a challenge. Can you commit to a short daily practice for a month? Two months? See what is reasonable for you and give it a shot.

Consistency over Quantity

Consistency is very important. When beginning or rediscovering meditation, we often jump in with a headstrong attitude. I know for myself when engaging in a new project or self-development exercise, I do this often and I need to carefully monitor myself. I get excited and set goals and expectations for myself. "This is important, and I am going to do this," I say to myself. I am notorious for setting goals each turning of the new year and other momentous dates with the expectation that "I am going to really do it this time around." This includes both activities and goals that I might not have succeeded in previously, as well as new endeavors. This is not bad in and of itself. The motivation to improve myself and be a better person or spouse or whatever is usually pure and authentic. But, particularly at the beginning, it is important to set small and realistic goals that can be accomplished on a regular basis.

This is particularly important with meditation practice. There is much spin about the positive impacts of meditation: Meditation will make you happier, less stressed, have higher academic performance, become more content, etc. Today it is not unusual for me to see a magazine touting the benefits of meditation or mindfulness practice on its cover as I check out at the store. And a basic underlying message of all of this is *you can be a better person than you are, these are the ways you can be better, meditation is the tool for doing this, and it is quite easy.* By absorbing this message, we can get ourselves into a very unproductive cycle if we set our goals too high. But if you start slow, with realistic and doable goals, your meditation practice will likely flourish. I have seen this play out time and time again with my students, and there are research studies that demonstrate the *frequency* of practice is a better indicator of success than duration.

To that end, a basic piece of advice is that *consistency is more important than quantity*. Start small, with very doable steps, and do these steps regularly over time. If you are like me, you may often set your goals too high. If a goal is not realistic and approachable then it is self-defeating. For instance, people often feel they need to meditate 20 to 30 minutes a day. This certainly might be beneficial, but not if it is not workable for you. It is very important to establish a goal that is realistic for you, one that you can do regularly over time. Thirty minutes a day, for instance, might not be realistic to you for several reasons. You simply might not be able to carve out the time, at least initially, on a daily basis. Or, like in some of my earlier experiences with the practice, this might simply be intolerable. I often recommend starting with five minutes a day in the beginning, and then once this becomes stable, to progress to longer periods.

The most important thing is to establish a regular practice that is realistic and workable in your unique situation. Having a short daily practice is much more effective, I believe, than not having a daily regular practice, and then putting pressure on ourselves to "catch up" with longer sessions. Habit is extremely important, and a short daily practice is the most effective way to promote lasting transformation. You will gain a level of accomplishment, which will fuel you to continue. If you become frustrated by either the duration or infrequency of your practice, then you are much less likely to return and continue regularly.

Recognize That Your Experiences Will Fluctuate

If you do a given meditation every day, say, for a week, you are likely to have a variety of experiences. Some days you may be totally into it and feel energized or transformed. Some days you may feel numb and like you are just going through the motions. Another day, you may be full of resistance and doubt. On still another day you might be so distracted that you literally cannot focus. All of this is normal and to be expected. The goal here is to develop an attitude of gentle perseverance. Just recognize this is normal and stick to your realistic commitment. When I teach meditation classes, it is very common for people to have powerful positive experiences when meditating as a group in class, but then to have other experiences when they meditate at home, or to report that their practice experiences varied dramatically over a week—and this is consistent with my own experiences. Again, the recommendation is to find something doable to you and stick with it regularly for an established period.

Don't Compare Yourself to Others

Don't compare your experiences to others, or even to your own expectations. In my own experiences, the comparing mind does not serve me well. It may be useful at times, but typically it hijacks my experience and does not allow me to live according to my true values. When stuck in the comparing mind, my world becomes constricted and I am often bombarded by self-criticism. This is a deeply ingrained habit for most of us and cannot just be wished away at once. I encourage you to recognize when this is occurring and try to give yourself a little space from its spell. This is particularly important for beginning meditators and can be a significant roadblock to progress. Your experiences are yours and yours alone, and there is nothing useful about comparing to others or to your own expectations of how these experiences *should* be. Most students I have worked with, if not all, experience the comparing mind. In terms of meditation, it serves no useful function whatsoever and we will work to loosen its grip through the *Wholesome Mindfulness* practices.

Ultimately, there is no one correct way to approach meditation. Your life and path are unique, and your approach to this material is authentically yours. Be gentle and kind to yourself and remember to be a scientist in the laboratory of your own life! Take what is useful for you in this book and leave the rest. And know that the more you consistently engage in the practices, the more you can reap the benefits of *Wholesome Mindfulness.*

Section 2

Coming Home To The Heart

Introduction to the Practices

In the next five chapters, you will be presented with three types of practices: (1) formal meditation practices, (2) self-reflective journaling activities, and (3) short embodied practices to be integrated into daily life. These three reinforce one another and deepen the possibility of transformation on the contemplative path. Below, each of these will be briefly introduced, along with general strategies for working with them throughout this book.

Formal Meditation Practices

You will first be introduced to various formal meditation practices. "Formal" indicates that you are setting aside a pre-specified amount of time to engage in the practice. You will be given instructions about posture, etc., as you proceed through the book. Typically, you adopt a preestablished posture you decide upon when engaging in formal meditation practice and follow a prespecified structure for each meditation. For beginner meditators, and even seasoned ones, it is very beneficial to utilize guided meditations. To that end, you can stream or download guided meditations at the book's website: www.dentgitchel.com/pursuingpurpose.

Self-Reflective and Journaling Activities

In most chapters, you will find one or more self-reflective or journaling activities. Like doing formal meditation practices, it is best if you set aside a specified amount of time for these activities. It does not need to be a long amount of time, but these are most effective if you are not also simultaneously engaged in other activities or taking in other information while doing these activities. Because many of us are constantly engaged in multitasking, this is a teaching and training in and of itself.

Short Embodied Practices

Each chapter also includes short embodied practices that can be adopted in the context of normal life. As such, they do not take additional time out of your day but offer you the opportunity to engage with your life in new and different ways. Many of these seem simple on the surface and may be easily overlooked. But in my experiences both as a practitioner and as a teacher, these offer an accessible opportunity to deepen the transformative power of contemplative practices and to bring their insights directly into our lives. This is particularly the case in our busy modern world. They allow us the opportunity to see meditation not as something divorced from everyday life but as something to be fully integrated into life. All of these practices, along with additional bonus practices, are included on the book's website: www.dentgitchel.com/pursuingpurpose.

To get the most out of these practices and the best opportunity for transformational effects, I recommend going through the practices and material methodically and systematically. Remember that when engaging on a path of meditation and contemplation we are developing new habits of body and mind. Just as we may build muscles and stamina through an exercise regimen, we are here building new attitudes and outlooks on life that build resilience, confidence, and purpose on the path of *Wholesome Mindfulness*. To that end, I recommend the following approach:

1. Commit to work with the practices and materials systematically on a regularly, preferably daily, basis. I recommend dedicating two weeks for each of the five upcoming chapters.
2. Keep a daily journal. A template for this can be found on the website at www.dentgitchel.com/pursuingpurpose.
3. Use this journal for the self-reflective activities and dai-

ly reflections on your engagement with the materials and practices.

4. Do the guided five-minute value-based intention meditation at the beginning of your day, also found on the book's website:

   www.dentgitchel.com/pursuingpurpose.

5. Do the longer meditations daily if possible, or at least several times throughout the week. This can be done in the morning with the short meditation or any time day or evening. There are one or two guided meditations included with each chapter.

6. Finish each day with the short value-based self-reflection, found on the book's website:

   www.dentgitchel.com/pursuingpurpose.

7. Do the embodied practices three to five times, or more, during each day. You will find several of these short practices in each chapter. These are indispensable for the full integration of the material into your life.

For those wanting to go deeper with this and other material, there are further resources available to you at www.dentgitchel.com, including additional guided meditations, online courses with me, and opportunities for personal guidance.

Chapter 4

Coming Home to Yourself

Coming home is a process of discovering who we really are. The first step involves tapping into our values and establishing a foundation of mindfulness. In many ways, we make our way through life as if we are sleepwalking, just going through the motions. Family, friends, educational systems, and the culture at large may have given you a long list of expectations about how you should live your life, but it may be hard to sift through all of this and find your own path. It may be difficult to have purpose and direction. Coming home to your values means cultivating and accessing your inner compass, which can be your guide through the complexities of life. This can help to awaken you from the confusion and lessen the anxieties you have likely experienced. Coming home is coming home to *your* values, which are the foundation of your unique path.

Without clearly defining our core personal values, it is difficult, if not impossible, to forge an authentic and purpose-driven life. Most of us have internalized a wide range of expectations and messages from external sources about how we should live our lives. It can be difficult to sort through all of this. On one extreme, we may become confused and directionless. On another extreme, we may succumb to the values and expectations placed onto us by others and develop a trajectory of life that is not authentically our own. At various points in my earlier life, I embodied each of these extremes. In order to access a true and authentic purpose for our lives, it is important to be able to identify and embody our own true and authentic core values.

Like all of us, you have been given many open and hidden messages about what to feel and not to feel, what to notice and not to notice, and what to think and not to think. And likely, the messages you have received have been conflicting. What is fake and what is real? Taking this all in, the *cowardly mind* becomes anxious and confused.

You might have reacted to this in a variety of ways. You may have rebelled against the messages and expectations that have been thrust upon you. You might have even rejected all authority. Or, you might have sought comfort and security in the traditions you have inherited. More than likely, you have vacillated between these two. Whatever the case, it is important to *wake up* more fully and to come home to your own values, intentions, and purpose. The more we tap into our authentic values, the more our lives have purpose.

Waking Up to Values, Intentions, and Purpose

An important step in the journey home is to find an inner compass and to return to it frequently—something that will point you in the right direction. The compass we need is a reflection of our own inner values. To forge a path, it is important that this path has a purpose and that this purpose aligns with our inner values. *Value* can be a very loaded term in our culture. You might associate it as something rigid and inflexible, or as something people beat you over the head with, implying that it is fueled by judgment and criticism. Value, as I use the term here, has a much different connotation. Think of it as what you hold most dear, what lies at the very foundation of your innermost desires; something so intimate that it might only be able to be shared with a select few.

From this lens, a value is an inner barometer—an inner sense—of what you hold most dear. It is important to understand this is not a moralistic approach. Values are fluid and subjective. What is true for me is not necessarily true for you. And importantly, *values are not rigid and fixed but may vary over time and in different situations.* Therefore, it is very important to be able to articulate your values and to be able to tap into them on an ongoing basis. Values give our lives direction and empower us to live in alignment with what is most true for ourselves.

When we are living in alignment with our inner values, we naturally discover more meaning and purpose in our lives. When purpose comes from within, it is authentic and powerful, which can provide us with previously unimaginable strength and determination. The more you are can live life according to your inner values, the more confident you will become.

Understanding Your Values

When approached from the authentic perspective of the *courageous self*, a value is the way we would truly like to be in the world. Values may express themselves to you in many forms. In my experience, I typically identify and activate my values through general intentional phrases or statements. For example, for the value of supportiveness: *to be a supportive father;* or for the value of kindness: *to be kind to others throughout the day.* My values often serve as wake-up calls for areas of my life that are currently being neglected. They are the guidelines and principles by which at the deepest levels I would like to live my life. As such, each functions as an internal compass pointing me back home.

Below is a list of possible values. This list is not exhaustive, and it is very important to reflect on values from your unique perspective and to articulate your core values in your own words. There is no right or wrong here. The point is to gradually gain the ability to identify and articulate the qualities you would most like to embody. These values can then serve as a compass toward home and help you to cultivate a life of purpose and meaning. Read over this list and write down four to five values that resonate with you, and feel free to add to the list. You can return to this type of inquiry again and again. Also, remember there is a five-minute value-based intention meditation that is fruitful to begin your day, as well as a short self-reflective value-based activity that can be a very transformative way to end your day, both found on the website: www.dentgitchel.com/pursuingpurpose.

Examples of Values

Acceptance	Devotion	Humor
Accountability	Discipline	Independence
Authenticity	Discovery	Innovation
Calmness	Easygoingness	Integrity
Collaboration	Enthusiasm	Joyfulness
Commitment	Even-mindedness	Kindness
Community	Faith	Loyalty
Compassion	Focus	Mischievousness
Cooperation	Freedom	Nonviolence
Courage	Generosity	Open-mindedness
Creativity	Gratitude	Patience
Curiosity	Hard Work	Practicality
Dedication	Humility	Productivity

Purpose	Responsibility	Strength
Reliability	Self-care	Supportiveness
Resilience	Service	Tolerance
Resourcefulness	Simplicity	Trustworthiness
Respect	Sovereignty	Willingness

Value-Based Inquiry

You will now have the opportunity to explore your own values. A key to this work is not to place expectations on yourself. Allow what emerges to emerge. Basically, you will be exploring the question, "What is most important to me?" This is a simple question, yet one that is very deep. And for most of us, this is a new way of self-relating. It is a way of self-relating based on respect and listening rather than on criticism and judgment. It is a way of self-relating based on trust in our inner wisdom. It is a way of self-relating that I did not learn until I was well into adulthood.

To better understand the areas in your life in which your values operate, the following self-reflective activity can be very helpful.

Self-Reflective Activity: Identifying Values That Are Important to Me and Why

Open your journal and prepare for a short journaling exercise. Now, take a few deep breaths and calm your mind and consider the following. Choose one or more of your core values to focus on in this exercise (remember this is an exercise that is fruitful to return to repeatedly) and ask yourself the following questions, spending a good bit of time with each question and articulating your response in full paragraphs.

- *What is this value?* Here, describe the value in detail: what it is and what its components are.
- *Why is this value important to me?*
- *In what areas of my life would I like for this value to manifest?* This could be education, work, family, friendships, recreation, volunteering in the community, etc.
- *In what ways do I currently embody this value?*

Just allow what emerges in your writing to emerge. Resist evaluation as much as possible. When done, go back and slowly read what you have written, allowing it to slowly be integrated into your mind-stream.

Actualizing Your Values with Intentions

Your values are guideposts that must be actualized with specific intentions. The meditation accompanying this chapter will allow you to tap into your inner values *and* to cultivate specific intentions stemming from such values. It is a good practice to come back to again and again. An effective intention should be specific and able to be actualized as actual behaviors. For instance, I might have a general value of *being supportive.* To fully actualize this value, however, I need to be able to actually embody it in my life. I need to be able to live it in concrete ways. Thus, it needs to be focused and refined. *I think of intentions as the path to embody our values.* An intention is a specific way that I would like for the value to live and breathe with me as I live my life. Thus, intentions following on my value of being supportive might take the form: *I will play basketball today with my son* or *I will sit and listen to my daughter as she tells me about her day.*

Reestablish Values Daily

It is helpful to return to our values and reestablish intentions again and again, ideally at least once a day. I find it remarkable how the ways that my values get expressed transforms over time, and how my intentions manifest differently on a daily basis. Gradually, our values and intentions can become the well from which we draw water all through our lives. They can serve as the foundation of everything that we do, both in the grand scheme of things and the prickly nuts and bolts of daily existence.

To assist in integrating them more fully into daily life, the following short embodied exercise can be extremely helpful. As discussed earlier, embodied exercises are very short exercises intended to be done in the context of busy daily life. They can be done amid the hustle and bustle of work, for example. Or, they can even be done during a quick bathroom break when visiting extended family. I do this short practice, for instance, before a stressful work meeting to help me maintain inner strength and balance.

Embodied Exercise: Embodied Values

- Take a moment to calm your mind by taking a few conscious breaths.
- Ask yourself, *"What is most important to me right now?" and "What value would I most like to embody?"* Sit with it for a few seconds and then ask the questions again.
- Breathe for a few moments and allow what arose to sink in, and then return to your daily activities with this value in mind.

This short and seemingly easy exercise can be quite powerful. For example, the other day I was about to enter a work meeting that I anticipated would become tense and stressful. I paused and briefly did this exercise before entering the meeting. By pausing and reflecting, I was able to see the bigger picture and the term *even-mindedness* came to me in my reflection. This planted a seed in my consciousness, and I was able to remain level-headed amid stress. If I began to feel tension arise within me or feel the urge to say something that I might regret later, I was able to remind myself of this value and to regain my sense of balance. To me, values are quite powerful and mysterious. If we are quiet and listen, our inner wisdom will help to direct us toward values that are important and appropriate for a given situation. And *mindfulness*, which we will turn to now, gives us a tool that enables us to return to our values in times of business or stress.

Waking Up to Your Sensations

Most of us live most of our lives in our heads, in the world of thoughts. We spend enormous amounts of time planning, worrying, examining, and the like. Does this resonate with you? This is very common. The result of this is that we often become divorced from what is actually occurring, both in the world at large and in terms of our own experience. We are literally living in our heads! Our lives may then become quite anxious. Meditation can return us to the world of our bodies and to sensing our actual experiences. As a result, we can become grounded in what is actually happening rather that what we think is happening or might happen. We can have much less anxiety and can encounter the world much more calmly and directly.

Mindfulness of Breathing

An effective way to do this is through mindfulness practice. The most popular and widely taught form of mindfulness is mindfulness of breathing, and this is my go-to practice, which I practice every day and is the foundation for all of my other practices. It has been researched extensively and has been shown to have many positive psychological as well as physical health benefits.

That said, I have found that even this type of practice, and its emphasis on stress reduction and relaxation, can actually wind us up if approached too rigidly. This practice can serve as a cornerstone and foundation of your life, as an anchor to help carry you through the ups and downs of life. And, one of the benefits of this practice is that *it is portable.* Wherever you go and whatever you are doing, it is available for you. Once you learn this practice and integrate it into your daily life, it can serve as a lifelong friend, a friend that continues to provide deeper levels of support and nurturance. As long as you are alive, you are breathing, and so you always have the opportunity to practice mindfulness of breathing.

Does Posture Matter?

Posture is a question that often comes up in meditation class, and so I will review a few recommendations here. First, it is important to take all recommendations with a grain of salt and to use your own experience and critical intelligence as guides. Only you know yourself and your body. Remember the advice to *be a scientist in the laboratory of your own life.* That said, here are a few time-tested suggestions:

- Comfort is important. You want to be comfortable enough to sit for a designated amount of time, and comfortable enough to be able to *relax.* If you cannot relax, you will not be able to meditate effectively.
- You also want to be *alert*, and to adopt a posture that contributes to alertness. Meditation is not ultimately about relaxation, but about *awareness.* To be aware, you need to be alert, and to adopt a posture that promotes this. Typically, the recommendation is to sit upright and have a straight back. Your back should be straight and upright but not rigid, allowing the skeletal system to support itself. If lying down, lie on your back in a position you do not associate with sleep, such as the *savasana* position from yoga, in which you are lying flat on your back with legs slightly apart and arms resting by your side in a comfortable position, with palms facing upward.

- In a nutshell, as one contemporary Tibetan Buddhist teacher suggests, the above recommendations can be condensed as *straight back and relaxed muscles.*
- Close your eyes or allow them to be very slightly open but not focusing on anything. Experiment and see what is most effective for you. Remember the basic suggestion is to be both *relaxed* and *alert.* If your eyes are slightly open, and you are sitting, allow your vacant gaze to rest gently downward at about a 45-degree angle.
- Allow the whole body to become as relaxed as possible, particularly the shoulders. Allow the shoulders to rest in a relaxed position that is not slouched.
- Allow the mouth to be slightly open and for the tongue to gently press against the roof of your mouth.
- If you are seated in a chair, allow your feet to rest flat on the ground beneath you. If you are seated on the floor on a cushion, make sure your knees are supported and there is not too much strain on your lower back.
- Decide what you will do with your hands during the practice. If seated, placing them palms down on your thighs is common, but there are many possible variations. Find what works for you. If adopting a lying position, hands can be placed to the side of your body or rest on your belly, or any other position that works for you.

- Take all instructions with a grain of salt. Try not to use this as another excuse to beat yourself up. The main instruction is to adopt a position that works for you, one that is conducive to both relaxation and alertness.

Below, I will provide instructions for basic mindfulness of breathing practice, and several guided meditations of various lengths are accessible on the book's website: www.dentgitchel.com/pursuingpurpose. The basic instruction is to follow the sensations of the body as you breathe. The breathing is allowed to be relaxed and natural. You are not forcing the body to breathe in any particular way but are allowing the body and the breathing to settle into its natural breathing patterns.

Options for Experiencing the Sensations of Breath

There are several options for following the sensations of breathing. I will review a couple of them here and suggest you pause for a minute or so with each option as you read this and explore it. Just pause and experience the sensations of the body as you gently inhale and exhale. One option is to observe the sensations of the breathing at or below the nostrils as you inhale and exhale. This is a popular method and one that I used almost exclusively for many years. A second option is to feel the sensation of the abdomen as it rises and falls during the breathing process, gently rising on the inhalation and falling with the exhalation. For many, this method can feel deeply grounding. A third option is to experience the sensations at the nostrils and abdomen simultaneously, I find that, for some, this encourages a more expansive and relaxing type of awareness. A fourth option is to allow the awareness to pervade the entire body and to experience the fluctuations of sensations throughout the body as you inhale and exhale.

Recognize, Relax, Release, and Return

I encourage you to explore and experiment with each of these methods and to have them as different tools in your toolbox. During any of the practices, the basic instruction is to simply be with the sensations of breathing as you inhale and exhale, one breath at a time. As you become distracted, as you naturally will, the instructions are simply to return to the sensations. I suggest using the 4 Rs approach I discussed earlier in Section One: Recognize, Relax, Release, and Return. Recognize that you have become distracted and that your mind has wandered. Relax and release your attachment to whatever it is that has drawn your attention away. And finally, return to the practice at hand.

Counting and Noting

You may find your mind wanders excessively and you feel you are unable to focus at all. Do not fret. There is nothing wrong with you. Your mind is just doing what it is trained to do.

Or, as one of my teachers sometimes says, "The brain just does what the brain does." A strategy here is to give your mind a small task while you are engaged in the formal practice. In essence, you are giving it something to do to keep it occupied. One strategy is to silently count each time you exhale from one to ten, and then begin again at one. When you lose count, simply begin again at one. A second strategy is to silently note the inhalations and exhalations. Silently note "inhalation" or "breathing in" as you inhale and "exhalation" or "breathing out" as you exhale. I still use this technique to this day when I am in a very stressful situation or a place of great anxiety and have difficulty calming my mind. And remember, these are all tools. Use them as they benefit you, and then let them go when they no longer serve their purpose.

Mindfulness as the Foundation

To me, mindfulness of breathing is a very foundational practice and one that I encourage you to return to time and time again. Remember the instructions on the importance of consistency. I am a firm believer in the benefits of short meditations done consistently. To that end, there is a five-minute version of this practice in the audio resources, as well as a longer 15-minute version, and a 30-minute version if you want to go deeper. And remember to not beat yourself up. And following from that, don't beat yourself up if you find yourself beating yourself up!

This "simple" practice of mindfulness of breathing prepares the foundation for us to become more mindful in daily life. Typically, we go through life ruminating, planning, and remembering, and not directly engaging with our sensations. This results in anxiety and operating predominantly from the *cowardly self.* When we are operating in this mode, we are on guard and defensive, even to our own experiences. Mindfulness practice allows us to access our *courageous self.* This approach is courageous because it involves being with whatever is present in a state of nonjudgmental awareness. Whereas the *cowardly self* is fearful and reactive, the *courageous self* is collected and in control. We can then be more in touch with what is really going on, including the needs of both others and ourselves. And this all begins by being present.

Embodied Exercise: Mindfulness in Daily Life

- Take an activity that you perform regularly, such as walking or doing the dishes. I do this daily while walking across campus to my office.
- As you perform this activity, simply be aware of the physical sensations.
- For instance, as you walk, feel the contact between your feet and the ground below, or of the overall motion of your body with each stride.

- Simply be aware of the sensations in your body as you perform this activity.
- Do this in short intervals, and then give yourself a break, and then come back. You are gradually retraining yourself to come back to the present.

Please note that all self-reflective activities, guided meditations, and embodied exercises in the book, along with bonus activities, are accessible at the book's resource page: www.dentgitchel.com/pursuingpurpose.

Chapter 5

Coming Home to Your Innate Goodness

"Innate" means that it is already there within you. Just as you have kidneys, lungs, and a heart within you, you also have innate goodness. Goodness indicates, among other things, strength, kindness, and compassion. Innate goodness means that at your core you possess courage, unconditional kindness, and pure compassion. This might sound hokey to you but it is not. This may run against the grain of everything that you have been taught but it is true, and you can verify it through your own experiences. It is there and you can discover it. In this chapter, you will practice skills to access these inner qualities and then to enhance and cultivate them. Just like muscles can be trained through exercise, these capacities we all possess can be developed. In fact, they can be developed beyond your wildest imagination. They are your birthright, even if you have never been told that.

Most of us were raised from a scarcity mentality and were taught to "go out and get our fair share." Life is a competition, and you need to go out and fight. Of course, survival is important, and most certainly there is a lot of conflict and violence in the world. This is not hard to see. Turn on the news. Listen to politicians. Log onto social media. What you see, it seems, is the triumph of the *cowardly self.* When our "leaders" prominently and consistently model and demonstrate the *cowardly self,* it trickles down to all of us. What trickles down is not prosperity or goodness, but psychological stench, cowardice, and fear.

We cannot help but absorb these messages of fear. If you are like me, they have been absorbed down to the very level of your cells and DNA. We have been brainwashed to think that we are *less than.* You have most probably digested this message throughout your entire life. It is impossible to be shielded from this ongoing negativity. You have been conditioned to view yourself in terms of how you compare to others and have been manipulated to believe there is something wrong with you that can only be filled through products, entertainment, and services. This is all a big lie, and we all suffer from this lie.

In the midst of all of this, it seems naïve to claim we contain innate goodness. But we do. And, you can verify this in your own experiences. I invite you to do just that.

You are more than this. I am more than this. We are all more than this. When teaching, I sometimes say that inside there is a buried nugget of gold that represents your innate positive qualities, rather than the inner turd you have been conditioned to believe in. Discovering your innate goodness is to reclaim what is truly yours. It is to come home to your inner nugget of gold. It is to come to who you really are, who we all are at our core.

When we tap into our inner goodness, we strengthen our confidence in the best aspects of our own humanity. We see that our true home is one of inner goodness. At times, we might get only a fleeting glimpse, and at other times a full-blown transformational experience. Eventually, however, we come to see that this inner goodness is not merely an experience but is us touching our very nature, the depths of who we are as living and breathing humans.

As you wake up to your own inner goodness, you are transforming the possibility of what it means to be fully human, to be truly yourself. Looking back, this is what I was truly after in all of my adventures. I was really searching for meaning, and nothing is more meaningful than coming home to innate goodness. And ultimately, believe it or not, you will come to see that the inner turd is a fake, a charlatan. Like a politician spewing filth, the inner turd is but a puppet. This part of you is the result of all of the false stories you have been told and have been absorbed into your psyche. It exists only because of the millions of times the wool has been pulled over our eyes. As you awaken to your inner goodness, however, the stench of the inner turd begins to fade until finally, it is barely detectable at all. What is left is your inner goodness, the nugget of gold at your heart, your true nature.

We have all strayed far from home and have lost our way back. My own life on the contemplative path has been full of bumps and bruises. By all accounts, I am a person of privilege. I am white in a culture that overvalues whiteness. I am male in a culture that continues to be patriarchal at its core. I am heterosexual in a culture that sees that as the model. Both of my parents have college degrees. I got accepted at an Ivy League institution. And yet, I emerged into early adulthood a psychological mess, full of self-doubt and existential angst. I portrayed a façade of being carefree and easygoing, but underneath, there was an inner turmoil that was deep and profound.

I carried this around as a secret inner burden and there were many times it nearly annihilated me. To this day, I say a daily prayer of gratitude that through the blessing of friends, the music, and community of the Grateful Dead, and my fortunate encounter with teachers and mentors, I was gradually able to fend off the spell of self-doubt and access my own inner goodness. Whatever self-doubt you may have, this is not who you truly are. Whatever your faults or anxieties, you have an inner goodness much deeper and more profound. Whatever your failures are, these do not define you. In Tibetan

Buddhism, your true nature—your inner goodness—is called *Buddha-nature.* I have it. You have it. We all have it.

Recognizing Unconditional Kindness

Have you ever experienced kindness with no strings attached? For many of us, we have not, and may find it unfathomable. Unconditional kindness wants what is best for another, with no strings attached. You might have been blessed to have received this in your family of origin, but most of us did not. Most often, in my experiences, the kindness we receive is often tinged with expectations. For instance, my grandmother loved me dearly and in many ways, I was her favorite. Her love for me was immense, and I am sure she said prayers for me daily. She had a very judgmental side to her, but this was largely reserved for other members of the family. I later came to see that even with her there was a strong set of expectations in her kindness toward me and I felt a lifelong burden to please her and to meet her expectations. I sometimes wonder how I got so interested in heart-centered practices and my reflections always bring me back to her. It is easy for me to bring up a strong feeling of gratitude when I think of her. And yet, her kindness was not completely unconditional. It was still tinged with judgment and expectation.

Most of us experienced deep hurts in our families of origins, and this makes it difficult—if not impossible—to understand that unconditional kindness exists, much less know what it is. And yet, it is part of who we fundamentally are as human beings. We have the right to receive it and are incomplete if we do not give it. Yet for the most part, we do not know how. I suspect this is one of the main reasons having pets is so important to many of us. Having a pet sometimes allows us the chance to to truly give and receive kindness. We may have had glimpses of it, but for most of us, experiences of both giving and receiving unconditional kindness have been relatively rare. You might not even believe it exists. But it does. The exercises below are here to help you access this innate quality of the heart.

Remember not to expect too much or to beat yourself up with expectations when you engage in the practices. Remember *why* you are doing this. Remember that any experience you have is authentic. Remember that you are developing habits, and habits take time. Remember to be gentle and friendly to yourself. Remember that you've got this!

The following exercise will allow you to reflect on experiences of kindness: times when you have been kind to others, times when you have been the recipient of kindness, and times when you have witnessed kindness. Like any of the self-reflective exercises in this book, this exercise can be done multiple times to enhance the deepening of your insights.

Self-Reflective Activity: What Are My Experiences with Kindness?

Open your journal and prepare for a short journaling exercise. A key to journaling is to suspend judgment as much as possible and to *let words flow* as smoothly and automatically as possible. Write slowly and deliberately in the absence of self-judgment, feeling the pencil or pen in your hand or your fingers on the keyboard. Breathe calmly and gently and simply allow your words to appear on the paper or screen of your device. I recommend doing this sort of exercise with a pen or pencil and paper, but that is totally up to you.

Now, take a few deep breaths and calm your mind and prepare for the following journaling activity:

- Ask yourself, *When have I been the recipient of unconditional kindness?*
- Hold this question gently in your attention and allow your reflections to emerge in your writing. If nothing comes to mind, include this in your reflections. Describe what comes up for you.
- How did it feel to experience this? In the body? In your thoughts and feelings?
- Describe as many experiences that come to mind (or you have time to explore).
- Now, take a few deep breaths and calm your mind.

- Ask yourself, *When have I expressed unconditional kindness to someone else?*
- Hold this question gently in your attention and allow your reflections to emerge in your writing. If nothing comes to mind, include this in your reflections. Describe what comes up for you.
- How did it feel to experience this? In the body? In your thoughts and feelings?
- Describe as many experiences that come to mind (or you have time to explore).
- Now, take a few deep breaths and calm your mind.
- Ask yourself, *When have I witnessed expressions of unconditional kindness between others?*
- Hold this question gently in your attention and allow your reflections to emerge in your writing. If nothing comes to mind, include this in your reflections. Describe what comes up for you.
- How did it feel to experience this? In the body? In your thoughts and feelings?
- Describe as many experiences that come to mind (or you have time to explore).
- Now, take a few deep breaths and calm your mind.

Embodied Exercise: Kindness in Daily Life

- Take a moment to calm your mind and center your heart by calmly breathing and reflecting on your inner values that are important to you right now.
- Reflect upon your current life situation.
- Quietly ask yourself, *How can I best express kindness to myself? To others?*
- Return to your breathing, allowing what you have experienced to settle into your mind, and resume your daily activities.

Cultivating Compassion

In terms of our innate goodness, kindness is only part of the story. While kindness involves wanting what is best for another, compassion involves desiring that they not experience suffering or difficulty. Consider true love as consisting of *both* unconditional kindness and compassion. From this perspective, compassion is very much the flipside of unconditional kindness. Whereas unconditional kindness is an expression of absolute goodwill, compassion is an expression of the desire that others not be harmed. In Buddhism, compassion is classically expressed as the wish that they be free from suffering.

I experienced this most viscerally for the first time when my daughter was being taken back to the operating room for surgery. I had been reading books on Buddhism for many years and had been engaged in compassion meditation for some time and felt I had a fairly strong understanding of compassion. My daughter was born with a hip condition that required multiple interventions and surgeries, beginning almost immediately after birth. In this one instance, the interventions she had received had not been successful, and so my wife and I had begun regular visits to Arkansas Children's Hospital for her to be treated by a physician there who specialized in the condition she experienced. As a result, she was to receive a surgical procedure more invasive than her previous interventions and I experienced fear and anxiety stronger than I ever had before. I literally felt I could not handle it but knew I must.

Throughout the morning, I said prayers and did whatever I could to try and have the courage to be present and face the situation. My wife and I waited with her in the pre-op area. She was about 19 months old and this was the first surgery where she was old enough to sort of know what was going on, and was crying and expressing her basic displeasure with this overall situation. As they wheeled her back to the operating room, she looked up at her mother and me and reached out and cried out for us, and then she disappeared through doors and was gone. At that moment, my heart burst open and there was a surge of strong energy that overcame my entire body and mind, and every ounce of my being was focused on her and her pain. There was an urge stronger than anything I had ever experienced to reach out and comfort and soothe her. If it were possible, I would have done anything to take her pain and discomfort onto myself and away from her. This is compassion. In many ways, it is our deepest expression of love and is highly misunderstood. It is not a weakness. In fact, it is an expression of our greatest strength and takes a great amount of courage both to actualize and to cultivate. An important part of coming home is accessing your own courageous heart—time and time again.

When I speak about compassion, I often begin with three statements: *Compassion is misunderstood. Compassion is not a feeling. The compassion cultivation process is paradoxical at every step of the way.* Now, let me explain what I mean.

In normal everyday language, I think we think of compassion as a strong feeling akin to sympathy. When defining compassion, I often hear people say it is "feeling sorry" for someone. There are certainly often strong feelings in a state of compassion, but sometimes they might be subtle or even not there at all. In strong states of compassion, such as the one I described above, there are certainly strong feeling components, but the strongest components of compassion involve strength, confidence, and factors other than sympathy.

There is often a sense of moving toward, an action-orientation to help. And sometimes there are thoughts such as, *"I should do this because it will be helpful."* In short, compassion is an overall orientation, a state of mind focusing on reducing the suffering or harm experienced by another (or our self). It is based on perception; a type of *seeing* that *knows* the other is suffering and a *relating* to this other in a very personal way. There are large and powerful experiences of compassion, like the one I described above for my daughter, and very small experiences, such as deciding to do the dishes so that it will in some ways reduce the stress of my spouse. It is basically an orientation of strength that meets the difficulties of the world as they are and attempts to respond with care, concern, and service.

There are many types of suffering, many types of stress, and many types of difficulty, and as such there are many types of compassion. I sometimes define compassion as *the ability to meet the difficulties of the world in a courageous and sustained and caring way.* It is not a weak state of mind. Rather, it is a state of mind of immense strength. It is based on courage and strength that we all innately have. We just have to tap into it and build it just like we build our muscles through exercise. The practices of *Wholesome Mindfulness* will help you to do just that.

The willingness to cultivate compassion is quite counterintuitive and paradoxical and is a sign of great courage. The fact that you are still reading this book shows me you have great strength and courage. We all do. But you have made a conscious effort to actualize yours. Firstly, meditation itself is counterintuitive. In our productivity-focused culture, disparaging comments are made about meditation, such as that it is "useless" or that all one is doing is "sitting around gazing at your navel," and you are constantly bombarded with messages that you should be useful and productive at all times. It takes courage simply to attempt to break free of the alluring sway and expectations of a mindless culture, and I applaud you for your insight and courage. In compassion practice, we are willingly engaging with the difficulties of life. What is more courageous and counterintuitive than that? And yet, it is also quite natural. This is because as you become more compassionate, you are coming home to who you really are.

Typically, we either resist difficulty wholeheartedly or become overwhelmed by it. This is deeply ingrained in us. We associate turning toward difficulty with distress, and so our default is to turn away from it. Why would we want to willingly engage with difficulty in meditation? Isn't meditation about relaxation and feeling good? I am often amazed when I offer compassion meditation classes to the community that people actually show up! And sometimes I feel a little guilty because I can sense that some people feel, "I did not sign up for this. I just want to relax and escape my troubles and you are asking me to think about them and engage with them!" Yes, my friend, the compassion cultivation process is counterintuitive and paradoxical, but in my experiences, well worth it. I would go so far as to say that it is indispensable in our ability to live healthy and engaged lives in the 21st century, and is necessary for the sustainable flourishing of the human species and planet at large. We all know this deep in our hearts.

The kicker in the paradox, as I often explain it, is that compassion also *feels good!* Developing a compassionate state of mind stimulates areas of the brain affiliated with emotional balance and happiness. The result is that you will become more resilient and emotionally balanced as your compassion increases. Strengthening the "compassion muscle" not only allows us to become better lovers, spouses, parents, friends, and citizens, but contributes to our own emotional and psychological health and well-being. And, a beauty in cultivating both compassion and unconditional kindness is that we not only strengthen their strength. You will be able to access these states more readily, to express them more clearly, and to express them in ways previously inaccessible or unimaginable. As you come home, the journey toward compassion and kindness becomes more natural and easy, and life becomes more meaningful and full of purpose.

The following self-reflective activity will help you to begin to get in touch with your innate compassion.

Self-Reflective Activity: My Experiences with Compassion

Open your journal and prepare for a short journaling exercise. A key to journaling is to suspend judgment as much as possible and to *let words flow* as smoothly and automatically as possible. Write slowly and deliberately, in the absence of self-judgment, feeling the pencil or pen in your hand or your fingers on the keyboard. Breathe calmly and gently and simply allow your words to appear on the paper or screen of your device. I recommend doing this sort of exercise with a pen or pencil and paper, but that is totally up to you.

Now, take a few deep breaths and calm your mind and prepare for the following journaling activity:

- Ask yourself, *When have I been the recipient of compassion?*
- Hold this question gently in your attention and allow your reflections to emerge in your writing. If nothing comes to mind, include this in your reflections. Describe what comes up for you.
- How did it feel to experience this? In the body? In your thoughts and feelings?
- Describe as many experiences that come to mind (or you have time to explore).
- Now, take a few deep breaths and calm your mind.
- Ask yourself, *When have I expressed compassion for someone else?*
- Hold this question gently in your attention and allow your reflections to emerge in your writing. If nothing comes to mind, include this in your reflections. Describe what comes up for you.

- How did it feel to experience this? In the body? In your thoughts and feelings?
- Describe as many experiences that come to mind (or you have time to explore).
- Now, take a few deep breaths and calm your mind.
- Ask yourself, *When have I witnessed expressions of compassion between others?*
- Hold this question gently in your attention and allow your reflections to emerge in your writing. If nothing comes to mind, include this in your reflections. Describe what comes up for you.
- How did it feel to experience this? In the body? In your thoughts and feelings?
- Describe as many experiences that come to mind (or you have time to explore).
- Now, take a few deep breaths and calm your mind.

Most of us in the modern world are very hard on ourselves. Our compassion for others may be more fully developed than compassion for ourselves. Developing self-compassion is very important, both for our own well-being and also to expand and strengthen our compassion for others. The following embodied exercise will help you to integrate self-compassion into your daily life.

Embodied Exercise: Self-Compassion in Daily Life

- Take a moment and calm your mind and center your heart by calmly breathing and reflecting on your inner values.
- Place both hands on the center of your chest as you breathe and reflect on what the situation in your life is. Ask yourself, *What difficulty am I currently experiencing?*
- Reflect that this difficulty is part of what it means to be human and no way reflects a deficiency or lack of self-worth on your part.
- Quietly ask yourself, *How can I best express compassion to myself?*
- Allow what you have experienced to settle into your mind-stream and resume your daily activities.

Please note that all self-reflective activities, guided meditations, and embodied exercises in the book, along with bonus activities, are accessible at the book's resource page: www.dentgitchel.com/pursuingpurpose

[illegible] Compassion [illegible]

- [illegible] and [illegible] center [illegible]
- [illegible] the [illegible] on the center of your chest [illegible]

[illegible]

Chapter 6

Coming Home to a Balanced Mind

Cultivating Confidence and Courage

You are now aware of the strength and courage involved in the journey home. I commend you on your journey. No longer lost, you have connected with your values, your heart, and your basic goodness. You have had at least a glimpse of the truth that has been hidden from you by the stories and narratives imposed on you by a culture interested in treating your life as a commodity, as something to be manipulated and valued in terms of its market value. This truth can be expressed in many ways. Maybe you resonate with the term *child of God.* Maybe *Buddha-nature* speaks to your heart. Or, maybe, *decent human being* captures your attention and speaks to your heart.

Isn't that ultimately what we are after? When we live according to our values, are grounded in the here and now, and live from the kindness and compassion of our innate goodness, we are then living life as embodied and decent human beings.

As you get more in touch with your innate goodness, you become stronger, kinder, and more compassionate. By this point, you may have had glimpses of this, or perhaps even more full-blown experiences. Whatever the case, you are right where you should be. Your journey is yours and yours alone, and your personal path home will gradually lead you to deeper levels of personal satisfaction, meaning, and purpose. Ultimately, the path home is not about grand experiences or meditative states but the ability to live through the ups and downs of life with dignity, from the core of our heart-centered values. As you work with contemplative practices you might discover that your values, compassion, or kindness are spontaneously emerging in daily life. This is not an aberration, but a sign that you have been doing the work.

It is not uncommon to feel that nothing is happening in meditation practice, and then discover there have been subtle changes occurring in normal daily activities and interactions. A student in one of my meditation classes coined the term "seepage" for this phenomenon. With a keen eye and the attitude of a scientist, you might observe the results of practice emerging—or seeping—into your life in subtle and unexpected ways. With our propensity for negativity bias, the ingrained tendency to notice threats and problems, and expecting the same old thing, again and again, it is easy to overlook these "small" occurrences. However, they are not small at all. The more we notice the positive, subtle effects of our practice, the more these are reinforced, and our confidence grows. Try to develop this keen eye with your own experiences. Is anything changing in the ways you relate to yourself? Is anything changing in the way you relate to others?

In a metaphorical sense, you are developing the muscle memory of your heart and your intentions. With practice, your heart and intentions begin to align in very small and subtle ways. Think of a musician or an athlete. Perhaps the musician trains for performances and the athlete trains for competitions. Along the way, however, are countless hours of repetitive training. A basketball player, for example, may work for long periods on footwork or shooting technique. The training may be very deliberate and mundane and feel very divorced from the actual game that is the ultimate goal of this training. The training may involve many setbacks and at times may feel very contrived and unnatural. Yet, one day it emerges in the context of a spontaneous action that is not contrived at all. A complex and precise set of footwork techniques is suddenly performed correctly in a very natural and uncontrived manner. To an outside observer, it looks spontaneous and natural. Yet, this fluid action results from many hours of practice and repetition. The hard work, the practice, "seeps" into the actual performance. Contemplative practices can work like that. By continually returning to your body, to your values, and to your innate goodness, these begin to "seep" into your actual life experiences.

For me, the proof of my practice arises in small and ordinary ways, often spontaneously; I notice that I have been slacking on chores and pick up my game, noticing the effects of my negligence on others. I give my son my full attention and read a book with him, even though my favorite basketball team is playing on television. I react to the person who aggravates me the most at work with kindness rather than aggravation. I notice a homeless person on the street, and approach and make eye contact rather than looking away. I spontaneously abandon a project that I am very attached to with my ego because it does not align with my deepest values. I take a few extra seconds and chat with someone at work even though I am busy and stressed. I do not check social media as much out of an act of self-kindness. I forsake a possible lucrative career path because it does not align with my heart. I noticed that I am grounded in my body and anxiety-free when speaking in public when normally I am a nervous wreck. Never underestimate these "small" victories, these small shifts in the way you live your life. I hear these types of stories time and time again from students in my classes on compassion, and they are true signs of progress.

Even if your formal practice of meditation is a struggle at times, the benefits will increasingly seep into your life in countless small ways. Early on in my contemplative path, I would rush to self-judgment concerning my practice based on the immediate effects of the practices (or my perception of them). However, after years of practice and ups and downs I don't do so much anymore. Meditation has become daily hygiene, like brushing my teeth. It is just something I do because I believe it benefits others and myself. I now believe wholeheartedly that the proof is in the pudding, and the pudding is in the ordinary activities and experiences in daily life. You might have noticed this in your own experiences. If not, I invite you to look. And, if you have, I encourage you to look again and again. You are a warrior of the heart. Just pause and take a look.

The following self-reflective activity will help you to access your confidence and courage.

Self-Reflective Activity: Courage and Confidence

Open your journal and prepare for a short journaling exercise. A key to journaling is to suspend judgment as much as possible and to *let words flow* as smoothly and automatically as possible.

Now, take a few deep breaths and calm your mind and prepare for the following journaling activity:

- Think back across your life and bring to mind an accomplishment you take satisfaction in. Don't put pressure on yourself to think of something big, but bring to mind something that brings satisfaction, ideally something that took effort and perseverance on your part.

- Write down reflections about this accomplishment. What obstacles did you overcome? Describe the effort you put in to achieve this accomplishment. Describe the supports you had during this process.
- Describe how you feel right now as you reflect on this accomplishment. How does it feel in your body? Describe the thoughts you are having.
- Now close your eyes and just breathe for a bit, allow the feelings of this experience to settle into your mind-stream.

The following embodied practice can be done in the context of a challenging situation in daily life. It is a way to tap into your inner courage and confidence on the spot.

Embodied Exercise: Courage in Daily Life

- Take a moment to calm your mind and center your heart by calmly breathing and reflecting on your inner values.
- Place both hands on the center of your chest as you breathe and reflect on what the situation in your life is.

Ask yourself, *What challenging situation am I currently experiencing?*

- Breathe into this experience and feel into what the challenge exactly is and what about it is difficult.
- Now recall another challenging life situation that you overcame. Recall how you felt during this challenge and then afterward. Tap into your inner courage, remembering other times when you have acted from a place of courage, and allow courage and confidence to fill your entire body.
- Take a few final deep and relaxing breaths and resume your daily activities.

Befriending Our Emotional Mind

Courage is an essential part of the path home. On the path of *Wholesome Mindfulness*, we inevitably bump up against our own thoughts and emotions and it takes courage to work with them effectively. Emotions are the driving forces in our lives and central to the things that give us both the most meaning and the most difficulty. What would life be like without emotions? To me, it is unimaginable. Emotions are central in all that we are, and it has taken me many years to fully recognize this. The degree to which we are unable to work effectively with emotions is the degree that we are unbalanced, and vice versa. Working with emotions, therefore, is central to the path of coming home.

Emotional balance means being able to understand our emotional lives and experiences and to make conscious decisions and actions based on our true values without suppressing what we are feeling. Let us take a quick look at emotions.

Thoughts

Thoughts and emotions are sometimes presented as distinct categories. However, thoughts can be an important entry point into the world of emotions. In fact, we sometimes think of thoughts as discreet forms of emotions, as the waves on the surface riding the deeper currents and tides of the emotions. They are two aspects of the same process.

I was in the gym recently exercising on an elliptical machine. I was minding my own business and listening to a favorite podcast. Suddenly, I heard a loud and annoying laugh coming from the space next to me. It distracted me, and I looked over and saw a person exercising and watching a show on his iPad. I recentered myself and continued exercising, chuckling at myself for getting annoyed. This occurred several more times and then I decided to block it out completely and just exercise. A little while later, I noticed a stream of thoughts such as, *"This guy is just like everyone else watching dumb sitcoms,"* and *"This is what is wrong with society. Everyone is so self-absorbed."* Thoughts like these were cascading in swiftly and I was consumed with negative evaluations of him and the world in general.

Waking up and remembering the instructions to be a *scientist in the laboratory of my own life*, I took a few breaths and just examined what was going on and what had happened. His behavior continued. Every minute or so, he would let out a loud and elongated—and to me, annoying—bout of laughter. Each time this occurred, I noticed in myself an instantaneous negative appraisal followed by a surge of anger, which was then followed by a surge of angry thoughts. For the remainder of my exercise session, I used this experience as a laboratory of sorts, exploring my anger response. This was a very safe and effective environment to explore this. The stimulus and my response occurred frequently and repeatedly, and there was nothing really at stake other than what I expected that my gym experience *should* be like.

This exploration of a seemingly insignificant experience at the gym opened my eyes to the relationship between reactive thoughts and emotions, and how easily and quickly I can get "hooked." Moreover, it was clearly evident that a "small" occurrence can quickly transform into a range of thoughts and emotions that affect our overall perception of everything that is occurring within and around us and propel us to act. Had I not noticed what was going on, I might have left there with simmering anger under the surface and a stream of negative thoughts about the world in general. Waking up and becoming more aware of our thoughts and thought patterns can be an effective and relatively accessible pathway into our underlying emotional states. Noticing and labeling them can be important in the process of coming home.

Recognizing Your Thoughts

There are many types of thoughts and thought processes. It is beyond the scope of this book to give an exhaustive list, yet you may find the following categories to be useful entry points for working with thoughts in the context of emotional awareness and the process of coming home.

Discreet Thoughts

Discreet thoughts refer to something very specific and easily definable. Examples of discreet thoughts might include thoughts such as, *"This is an apple," "Bob is an asshole,"* or *"I need to go the store to get some milk."*

Narrative Scripts

We spin many stories about our self and the world around us. A friend and meditation teacher of mine refers to these as "selfing." It is like we are going through life with an ongoing metanarrative occurring, like a sportscaster giving a play-by-play analysis of our lives. I don't know about you, but this rings very true to me. Stories about myself include: *"I am an introvert and do not like large crowds," "I never get a fair deal," "Dent, you never get anything right,"* and *"I will be persecuted if I become vulnerable in public situations."* It is very informative to notice and label these types of thoughts, particularly thoughts or themes that are recurring. For me these thoughts sometimes manifest as *I statements* and other times as *you statements*, as if an eternal observer is watching my life.

For instance, one of the themes that emerges when observing my thoughts I have labeled *catastrophic Dent.* The theme of this type of thought is that failure will come from whatever endeavor I am involved in and that calamity will result. With repeated observation, I have realized this type of narrative is based on fear and is motivating me not to act on whatever I am engaged in. If I do not recognize what is going on, fear will hijack everything else and rule the show and I will *react* based on this largely unconscious fear reaction. However, if I wake up and notice *catastrophic Dent* when he arises, I can get some space between my thoughts and myself and thus between the underlying emotions and these thoughts, and then I can have much more choice and autonomy in how to respond.

Internal Rules

These types of thoughts are a little deeper and more difficult to uncover, and are closely linked to our core emotional responses. They are closely tied to deeply held internal wounds, or in ways that our needs have not been met or have been inhibited. They are approached differently in different therapeutic models. According to Virginia Satir, a prominent family systems therapist, they are expressed as *rules* and manifest using the terms *never* or *always*. For instance, if you grew up in a household in which you were not allowed to express anger, you might have internalized a rule that *"I must never express my anger."* If you were always pushed hard to succeed, then you might have internalized a rule that *"I must do everything perfectly."* If the adults who raised you projected their unmet need for happiness onto you, you might have internalized the rule that *"I am always responsible for the happiness of others."* If you were told or you experienced that the world of emotions was a scary place, you might have retreated to your head and developed a rule of *"I must never trust my feelings."*

These are unique to each of us and there are countless variations and subvariations. What they all share in common is that in some ways they propel us to gravitate toward certain aspects of our experiences and to minimize or ignore other aspects of our experiences. And consistent with a major theme from this chapter, a result of this is a reactionary and emotionally unbalanced mindset.

Emotional Activation

Like our evolutionary ancestors, we constantly take in our surroundings as we are going through life. I sometimes think of humans as scanning devices. We go through life constantly scanning the environment for cues that there is something important going on. Suppose we detect a threat. This immediately registers in the brain as something *important.* In other words, signals are sent to the brain that this deserves more attention. A second appraisal is then made as to whether this phenomenon *matters.* In other words, *What is at stake in this encounter with something that has been deemed as important?* If nothing important is at stake, then we may lose interest and proceed with life. However, if something is at stake, then the emotional system may be mobilized. In the case of a threat, what is at stake? Is it safety of self or loved ones? Thus, this ingrained appraisal mechanism is constantly on the lookout for what is important and what is at stake, which is how an emotional response can be triggered.

The Lenses of Emotions

As indicated, once something is assessed as being at stake, the activated emotional system takes on a life of its own. You can verify this with your own experiences. Once you are in the grip of a strong emotion, you are often taken for a ride. One of the first steps in a *Wholesome Mindfulness* approach to emotions is to recognize when this is occurring, and in the modern world this is almost all of the time. As we are bombarded with stimuli, our emotions are being triggered in rapid cycles that have never been experienced previously in our evolutionary history. The phrase *blinded by emotions* gets at this experience of being overtaken by the energy of the emotional system.

When the emotion that is triggered takes the driver's seat and overcomes us, psychologist Paul Eckman refers to this as the *refractory period.* I refer to this period as being captured in the *lens of emotions.* Our objectivity, to the degree that we have it, is sacrificed and we see the world through the lenses of the emotion in charge. For instance, when you are angry, you are seeing the world through the lenses of your anger goggles. When you are disgusted, you are seeing the world through the lenses of your disgusted goggles. When you are afraid, you are wearing your fear goggles. When you are excited, you are wearing your excited goggles. When you are lustful, you are wearing lust goggles, and on and on.

You get the picture. But, so what? Here is the kicker: The more you are enmeshed with the emotion, the more you have given up your autonomy. You have, to a large extent, given up your ability to see things clearly and to make choices. There are, of course, gradations to this, but in essence, the lens of the emotion often blinds us to what is truly going on and inhibits our ability to perceive, think, and act clearly. The emotion literally reinforces itself by seeing what it wants to see and ignoring what it does not want to see. For instance, when you are wearing anger goggles, you literally perceive things in the environment to validate that anger and ignore cues that your anger might be misplaced.

For me, not being aware of this can cause me to act in ways that are contrary to my true values. When I first began to work explicitly with emotions in my meditation practices, this point was brought home to me very clearly. I was watching my six-year-old son play soccer at practice, just watching and enjoying a pretty day and loving and appreciating life. For some reason, I decided to check my email, an example of a very simple way we often distract ourselves. I read an email from my boss that triggered my anger. I put my phone away, probably aware of some psychological discomfort, but probably unaware that my anger had been triggered and that I had put on my anger goggles. A while later, I found myself in a fit of rage. A kid on the team had gotten hurt after being kicked by another player during practice. In my mind, I was rehearsing scenarios of how I should act based on my anger. I noticed thoughts such as: *"Kids are always getting hurt. The coaches should be doing a better job supervising what is going on," and "This is a very poorly run organization. I think I need to send an email and notify them of this," and "That kid who did that is always hurting other kids. Someone needs to talk to his mother."*

The emotion had hijacked my ability to see clearly. I had on my anger goggles and was seeing the world through its lenses.

And importantly, I was primed to act. Luckily, I *woke up*. If I had not, I likely would have sent a nasty email or gotten other people involved and created a drama that I later would have regretted. To wake up is to wake up to the fact that we are wearing goggles and to choose whether to wear them or not, or at least to recognize that we are wearing them and to choose whether to act or not in accordance with our true values. It is difficult to do and an ongoing process, but one that yields immense benefits. As we wake up, we gain power and control in our lives that allow us to follow our true path.

For me, the practice of meditation and gaining clarity often feels like waking up from a sleep of sorts. For instance, even in basic mindfulness of breathing practice, when I notice that my mind has wandered or has been hijacked, it is not as if I have calmly and objectively watched it wander away. Now, I wake up with a moment of clarity and notice this has happened. And waking up amid a strong emotion is similar. Ideally, I would notice the moment an emotion has been triggered and then make a conscious decision whether to follow its lead. But often, this does not happen. I might wake up already under the grips of the strong emotion, or worse yet after I have already acted out.

The Logic of Emotions

Each emotion and emotional experience has a logic of its own, and importantly, the logic motivates us to act in a particular way. The lenses of the emotion present us with a skewed vision of reality that propels us with the impulse to act to reinforce the logic of that emotion. This is not to say emotions are not useful, necessary, and beneficial, but that when they operate automatically, we become *reactive* and lose our autonomy, and in doing so, become estranged from our innermost values. And each time we do so, we become further lost and farther away from home.

The logic of an emotion tells us to view the world in a specific way that reinforces its own logic, which is propelling us to act. For instance, anger perceives an obstacle between us and something that we want or something that we hold dear and propels us to act to remove this obstacle. Fear perceives a threat and pushes us to fight or flee. Disgust perceives an invasion of something toxic and tells us to remove this intruder. Excitement perceives something desirable and drives us to attain the object of our desire, propelling us into the cycle of addiction.

The Problem with Emotions

It is important to note that this is not a criticism of our emotions and our emotional experiences. Our emotions serve very important functions. For instance, your fear instinct can alert you to real and present dangers. However, in the modern world, this fear is triggered again and again in very unproductive ways, and we are unable to articulate both what we are actually feeling and how what we are experiencing is propelling and motivating us to act. We are simply not hardwired to deal with all of this. This can result in overwhelm and triumph of the *cowardly self.* But this is not the final story. We. Can. Wake. Up. And the more you wake up, the better you will be able to have choice, freedom, and contentment in your emotional life.

Shades of Emotions

We often only notice our emotions when they are strong and powerful. However, when we pay attention, it becomes apparent there are many shades to our emotions. Consider anger for a moment. Anger is most apparent when it becomes strong and our "blood boils over." But there are many shades of anger; for example, slight irritation or aggravation. These subtler shades of emotions are easily overlooked and deemed as unimportant. But they have great impacts on our lives. These subtler shades of emotions can skew our sense of reality, can prime the pump for larger emotional outbursts, and can draw us away from our inner values and innate goodness. However, through the tools of mindfulness, you can become more emotionally balanced and able to accurately assess the shades of emotions you are experiencing.

The following embodied exercise can help you bring mindfulness to your own experiences during daily life.

Embodied Exercise:
What Am I Feeling and Thinking Right Now?

This is a very powerful and helpful short embodied exercise to do frequently during your daily activities. It helps to build emotional literacy and to bring a little bit of space and awareness to your emotional life.

- Take a moment to calm your mind and center your heart by calmly breathing and reflecting on your inner values.
- Place both hands on the center of your chest as you breathe and reflect on what the situation in your life is. Ask yourself, *What am I feeling and thinking right now?*
- Now, simply breathe into your experience. Do not force anything, just allow your awareness to gently observe your experience. Silently note for yourself what experience is occurring.
- Quietly ask yourself, *How is this emotion causing me to view the world?*
- Is this emotion motivating me to act? How?

Allow what you have experienced to settle into your mindstream and resume your daily activities.

The Swirl of Emotions

Strong emotions do not exist in isolation. They emerge, at least in my own experience, from what I call the *swirl of emotions.* When reflecting on the life of emotions, I often think of the State Fair of Arkansas, a place that I visited annually during my childhood. This was not a polished and flashy amusement park like you might find in Southern California or Florida, but a place with rickety rides that squeaked and creaked, corn dogs, cotton candy, livestock, and every delectable and putrid smell imaginable. Unimaginable wonders and filth assaulted the senses from every direction. It was unpolished and real and captivated my young mind. My own work with emotions reveals the world of emotions much like this.

In the modern world, our emotions are swirled together and triggered at mind-boggling speeds and in hitherto unimaginable ways. Through social media platforms, political manipulation, rapidly changing and increasingly invasive forms of technology, entertainment, ingenious and self-serving advertisements, and fast-paced consumer and service-driven economies, our sensations and emotions are bombarded and triggered to react in exponentially increasing rates. We are forced to live and function in a world for which we are not designed nor hardwired. This is not the world I grew up in, and it continues to advance and change by the minute. The good news is that we have the tools to manage this. Through mindful awareness we can gently cultivate the ability to understand the range of emotions we are feeling and the various lenses through which we are seeing the world, and come home to a place of emotional balance.

Layers of Emotional Experience

In addition to the swirl of emotions are underlying layers to our emotional experiences. When I am angry, for instance, and sit with my anger willfully and compassionately, a deeper level of hurt or abandonment might emerge. If I am experiencing nervousness or anxiety about public speaking and am able to really see what is going on, there might be a deeper level of shame or insecurity. Or, underneath my fear might reside a deeper level of sadness. I refer to each of these as the *core emotional experience* that might underlie what is on the surface. Being aware of these can be very liberating personally and can help us to more effectively develop empathy and compassion for others.

Importantly, we also have emotional reactions to our own emotional experiences. You may have learned that anger is not appropriate or is something to be afraid of. As such, when you experience anger, you may quickly react to this with shame or fear, with the latter emerging as the dominant emotion. In my own work with anger, for instance, I have been very surprised by the awareness that I am very afraid of being the recipient of another's anger. I had thought I was pretty in touch with my anger and have been trying to work with it more effectively for many years. But this new realization was quite eye-opening. I have noticed that this fear, when it emerges, is quickly pushed aside and a variety of more pleasant emotions emerge that allow me to detach from the fear and to avoid the perceived anger and displeasure of others. This strategy of reactive emotions probably emerged in early childhood and likely served me in very useful ways. However, this process is largely counterproductive in my adult life. It has inhibited my ability to work effectively with the underlying fear and to move through it. And, in turn, this has inhibited my ability to follow my heart and successfully pursue some of my deepest yearnings and meet the challenges that life presents. We are each unique, but the process of recognizing the layers of our emotional experiences can be an important part of the coming home process for us all.

Holding our Emotions in Courageous and Compassionate Awareness

Cultivating a state of compassion for ourselves helps us to be with whatever emerges in a clear and nonreactive manner, including our own experiences and emotions. Whereas problematic emotions blind us, in varying degrees, to what is actually going on, compassion allows us to see clearly. We might say that compassion goggles are clear, whereas the various emotional goggles all have degrees and shades of tint.

Compassion allows us to perceive correctly what is going on both in our selves and in others and to respond effectively and authentically.

The lens of compassion allows us to truly be with our emotional experiences. Compassion gives us the ability to hold our difficult emotions in awareness, and yet not to be overcome by them. Cultivating compassion can give you the ability and courage to explore your emotional terrain and to gain new levels of emotional awareness, balance, and literacy. Compassion can give you the strength to be with your own difficult emotional experiences in a sustained and caring way. The potential transformations of this cannot be overstated. With compassionate awareness you can learn to be less reactive and to navigate the swirl of emotions with clarity, commitment, and strength. Coming home to our emotional minds can give each of us the freedom to come home to a sense of belonging amid the confusing modern world. You can come home to your own autonomy and ability to choose and respond wisely. And, in doing so, you can live life according to your deepest values even in a "world gone mad."

Navigating Difficult Emotions

All emotions serve a purpose. They have adapted through evolution to help us to survive and to protect us. Moreover, many of our individual reactionary emotional patterns evolved during childhood and served important functions. From this perspective, there are no "good" or "bad" emotions. Certainly, some emotions appear to be more inherently pleasant than others, but that is not to say the unpleasant emotions are bad. However, many of our emotional experiences become problematic for various reasons: One, as we have seen, habitual and reactive patterns may have emerged that inhibit our ability to function optimally and to live in accordance with our deeper inner values. Two, the emotions may be triggered in modern contexts that are inappropriate. In other words, the emotional patterns emerge in contexts in which they are not useful. And three, the emotions themselves may be so strong, forceful, and overpowering that we do not have the tools to work with them skillfully. Below are *some* emotions that might be difficult for you. This is not an exhaustive list, but one that can hopefully serve as a reference point in your own development of emotional literacy and balance. It is very helpful to begin to recognize the goggles you are wearing and the lenses you are seeing the world through.

Anger

Anger emerges when something gets between us and something that we want. It stimulates us to act to remove the obstacle between our desired object and us. It propels us forward to move and remove. In reference to your own experiences, the object of anger can be an unpleasant emotion or other internal experience that blocks your experience from a more pleasant emotion.

The following self-reflective activity will help you to gently touch into your anger and notice its effects on you.

Self-Reflective Activity: Anger

The task of working to understand our distinct emotions and how they impact us can be very helpful and contributes to the development of emotional literacy and balance.

For this journaling activity, suspend judgment as much as possible and *let words flow* as smoothly and automatically as possible. Write slowly and deliberately, in the absence of self-judgment, feeling the pencil or pen in your hand or your fingers on the keyboard. Now, take a few deep breaths and calm your mind to prepare for the following:

- Reflect back on your recent past. Bring to mind a time or two in the recent past when you have felt and/or expressed anger.
- Describe the situation(s). What was going on around you? In your life?
- Describe the arc of the anger. For instance, did it come on fast or slow? Go away quickly or linger?
- Describe how the anger felt in your body. Be as specific as you can.

- How did the anger cause you to see yourself, others, and the world around you?
- How did the anger motivate you to act?
- Did this emotion serve you? How?

Fear

Fear emerges when we feel threatened. According to the classic *fight or flight* fear response, it propels us away from danger and to safety. It is affiliated with the same primal emotional system as anger and is largely at the root of the *cowardly self.* In reference to your own experiences, fear can even be triggered when emotions or other internal experiences appear to us as threatening. This can be due to a variety of reasons, including childhood experiences, social or familial expectations, or emotional illiteracy. For example, I have struggled with a fear of success or accomplishment because somehow in my life I absorbed the message that success and accomplishment are selfish and therefore bad. Or, someone might be afraid of anger if they were given the message that anger is bad and should not be expressed.

Envy/Jealousy

Envy and jealousy emerge when we see that others have something that we wish we had. To most of us, these emotions feel very unpleasant and are difficult to sit with or acknowledge. This is especially the case, maybe, for those of us who have done a lot of meditation or "inner work." These emotions, in fact, can tell us very important information about something we truly want in our lives and, in my experience, can help us tap into our deepest inner values. When these arise, if you can sit with them and use them as tools for self-exploration, they can be very transformative and beneficial. For instance, my own jealousy and envy of respected colleagues and friends who had written books was an important message to me that I really wanted to write a book.

Disgust

Disgust is a powerful—and often overlooked—emotion. Even in contemplative circles, it receives little attention. However, it is at the root of much of our compassion and empathy deficits both in society and toward ourselves. Disgust occurs when we perceive something as *toxic*, and its logic is that *this toxicity, or poison, must be removed.* When we are wearing our disgust goggles, the other is dehumanized and compassion and true kindness are basically not possible. In terms of society at large, it is probably the most dangerous emotion and is easily and willfully manipulated by politicians and propaganda machines. It can motivate us to act in very cold and calculating ways. Though unpleasant if felt and experienced on a deep level, on the surface it can be quite enjoyable, as it may convey a sense of power and superiority. In reference to your own experiences, disgust can emerge when emotions or internal experiences arise that you find hard to swallow and that elicit shame. For example, I may have been conditioned to believe that lust is morally wrong and feel self-disgust when it appears.

Resentment

Resentment is a kind of cold anger that emerges when we have been repeatedly harmed by someone or some institution, or when we have been harmed so very deeply that we *cannot get over it.* It can motivate us to get out of a harmful situation or to take or want to take revenge. As such, it can serve a very liberating function that can provide strength to leave an abusive situation in which we have been legitimately harmed. However, it can be very toxic if it is held onto after it has served its purpose. In a state of resentment, the heart is closed, and this may be experienced as *tightness* in the chest region. It can be a very difficult emotion to sit with, but can convey important information about ways we have internalized actual and perceived harm done to us. I have been amazed to discover how I have carried past grudges with me for many years. It has been for me a difficult emotion to work with; for one, because it is unpleasant, and second, because the hurts themselves are real. There is a sense of moral superiority of holding onto the resentment, but the relief of released resentments has been quite profound. In reference to your own experiences, it can shine light on very important aspects of yourself that are worthy of forgiveness and self-compassion.

Excitement

This may seem like a strange emotion to include in this list, but I believe it is very important. Contemplative researcher Paul Gilbert identifies three major emotion and drive systems: First, there is the threat system affiliated with the *lizard brain* and *cowardly self*. Second, there is the drive system involved in acquiring resources such as food or sexual partners. And third is the compassion system affiliated with our mammalian brain and the *courageous self*.

The second system is often overlooked, yet it drives much of our behavior in a consumer-driven society and is the system out of which excitement emerges. Excitement emerges when we are actively seeking something we desire, and motivates us to acquire it. This may be most evident in a moment of lust, but in my own observations, it motivates a lot of our modern behavior. For instance, purchasing items online may provoke excitement, thus providing us with a buzz that can be quite addictive. The excitement lenses are activated frequently and reinforced perpetually. It is quite problematic, at least partly, because it can never be satisfied.

Like all reactive emotions, it skews our perception of reality and causes us to see the world that is self-reinforcing. And once this self-reinforcing feedback loop is set into motion, it is difficult to stop, much less to recognize. However, it likely takes you further and further away from your true inner values. It manifests in, among other ways, constant preoccupation with distraction, entertainment, sexual stimuli, and resource acquisition. In reference to your own experiences, it can also emerge as an antidote to the above difficult emotions that we do not want to experience. We often flee here to avoid what we don't want to feel there. For instance, I might feel a lot of anxiety due to world events and then attempt to suppress this anxiety by inducing excitement. However, when done reactively, the result is often that we stray further and further from our true inner values, compassion, and unconditional kindness. For me, the process of coming home involves being aware of this desire for excitement, the difficult emotions I may be avoiding, and the effects of this avoidance on my own mental and psychological health.

Please note that all self-reflective activities, guided meditations, and embodied exercises in the book, along with bonus activities, are accessible at the book's resource page: www.dentgitchel.com/pursuingpurpose

SECTION 3

Coming Home to the World

Chapter 7

Mindfulness in the Modern World

At this point, you may be well along on your journey home. You might have a greater sense of your core values and have developed your capacity for mindfulness. You might have tapped into innate unconditional kindness and compassion that you did not know were there. You might have new and deeper understandings of your emotions and your emotional life. If this is so, rejoice and let this sink in. Allow the progress you have made on your journey home to expand into your heart and into your mind.

Now we will bring the tools of *Wholesome Mindfulness* into the complex modern world of relationships and communication. In many ways this is uncharted territory. The world as we know it changes and becomes more complex at mind-boggling speeds and does so in an exponential manner. There have always been generation gaps, but now the gaps are perhaps greater than ever before and occur much more quickly. Thinking back to my childhood, it seems like it was another universe that I inhabited from the one I live in now. For contemplative practices to be relevant in the modern world, it is important for them to be able to apply to the intricacies of the modern situation. It is one thing to be aware of my thoughts and feelings and to have a greater sense of my capacity for compassion and kindness, but quite another thing to be able to fully implement these in the complex modern world.

As we make progress on the journey home, it is natural for our perspective to change and for us to be able to look at our relationships and ourselves from new perspectives. Think back to an earlier time in your life. Recognize how your perspective has changed, how your views and perspectives have matured and transformed. In a very significant sense, you are the same person you were then. You are connected to your past self through a continuity of life experiences and memories. And yet, in another sense, you are not the same person. Your current perspective has *transcended* that of your past self. In some ways, your current perspective is probably more accurate and reflective of reality than your past self. For a silly and obvious example, think back to a time in childhood when you believed in Santa Claus. To the child, Santa was *real.* But as you matured, this perspective was transcended.

Though much subtler, the path of spiritual transformation in general, and *Wholesome Mindfulness* in particular, is like this. Our previous views are gradually transcended, and we open ourselves up to newer experiences and perspectives, and these are increasingly more valid, wholesome, and reflective of the way things really are. The process of coming home is *both* about learning new skills, mindsets, and behaviors and unlearning and transcending past perspectives.

Reimagining Progress

There is always a tension between how *things actually are* and how *we perceive them to be.* Basically, as we begin to wake up on the journey home, we begin to understand ourselves very differently. I think this is evident to any of us after we have undergone any type of growth or development process. We see ourselves differently after a growth or change process. We can look back and say that the way we were viewing reality was somehow flawed.

Perhaps you have experienced this while reading this book and doing the exercises. As we become transformed on our own personal journeys home, we are undergoing, among other things, a process of unlearning. Maybe you now experience your relationship with your emotions differently. When we are emotionally illiterate, we tend to identify with our emotions and live very reactively without even knowing we are doing so. Maybe now you have a little more spaciousness, awareness, and choice in terms of responding to your emotions. To the extent this has occurred, you now have a slightly transformed relationship with your own mind and emotions, which means you have a transformed understanding of yourself.

You might now have a deeper understanding of your most important values and your innate capacities of compassion and unconditional kindness. Perhaps you now have more direct insight into your mind and your bodily sensations. Perhaps you now have tapped into internal capacities of confidence and courage that you did not know you possessed. Perhaps you have always identified predominantly with your *cowardly self* and now this identification has loosened and softened somewhat. Perhaps now you have even begun to identify, if only in glimpses, with your *courageous self.* To the degree that any of these are true, you now have a new and more accurate understanding of your *self.*

Congratulations!

The journey home is not an all or none process. Often, in our modern culture we put so much pressure on ourselves to be perfect or to get things right. We tend to push ourselves hard or take the opposite extreme and give up completely. In this constant striving to be better, to achieve, we tend to overlook what is really going on, including progress we might have made. Recognizing more authentically your relationships with your thoughts, emotions, values, and other internal qualities is amazing progress. You may have overlooked this on your own journey home. We tend to approach journeys and endeavors with a linear mindset: There is an endpoint, and we have succeeded when we arrive at the endpoint. Success is achieved by reaching the desired destination. This journey, however, does not operate from that framework.

In a very real sense, the journey itself is the goal. The journey home largely involves deeper levels of understanding and awareness. We have already explored this and you have already experienced this. As you have become more in touch with who you really are, your sense of self has shifted. The shift does not have to be dramatic. We sometimes think of meditation experiences as necessarily involving profound and dramatic transformations. From the *Wholesome Mindfulness* perspective being offered here, that approach is at best misleading and at worst harmful. It is misleading because real and true transformation typically does not occur is such ways. It can be harmful because it misrepresents the actual processes that occur on the contemplative path home, which can actually inhibit our ability to come home to our own lives. Our lives are messy. The world is messy. The path home helps us sludge through this messiness with more insight, purpose, and courage than we have otherwise. We learn to be better friends to ourselves, and ultimately, to be better friends to others.

Reimaging your Relationships

As you come home, you begin to view your life through the lenses of mindfulness and compassion rather than through the lenses of emotional reactivity. As such, your ability to authentically engage others and the world increases. This is a very important observation and one that is critically important to reflect on. *Wholesome Mindfulness practices do not involve retreating from the world and from the messiness of life. On the contrary, they call us to engage in the world in new and wiser and more resilient ways.* As we learn to distance ourselves from the *cowardly self*, which is based on a perspective of fear and isolation, we gradually learn to have healthier and more authentic relationships not only to our inner values, qualities, and capacities, but also with others who we share the world with. A perspective of *Wholesome Mindfulness* helps us to be more authentic lovers, friends, colleagues, and basic citizens of the communities we inhabit. Ultimately, meditation is not about leaving anything, but about returning to everything fully—that is, at least to everything that is important.

In neuroscience research there is something called the *default mode* or *default network*. A lay interpretation of this is how the brain operates when we are not doing anything else. One method of studying the brain and its functioning is to study what occurs when a subject is engaged in some task or project of interest. To study the *default mode*, a very different approach is taken. Basically, a participant is told to do nothing and then brain measurements are taken in this state of non-doing. The results are quite interesting. Basically, the "me" parts of the brain are involved, including the medial prefrontal cortex, posterior cingulate, lateral parietal cortex, and hippocampus. These are parts of the brain associated with primal survival instincts, largely corresponding to what I call the *cowardly brain*. Basically, in this state, our conscious awareness and processing are being constantly stimulated by the primal fight or flight system. When "doing nothing," persons operating from this default state have a lot of anxiety and tend to be preoccupied with rumination and worry. I can definitely relate to this. Can you? For instance, when I am at a stoplight, my mind can sometimes take off on a flight driven by worry and anxiety if I'm not being mindful.

An exciting fact is that the default mode of operating can actually be transformed through basic mindfulness meditation practice. In as little as eight weeks, the brains of beginning meditators have been shown to change. When operating in the default state, sitting and "doing nothing," the parts of the brain that are being activated and used actually change. Whereas before stress and worry were being stimulated, now the parts of the brain being stimulated involve the less-used sensory pathway systems. As the part involved with conscious awareness, the prefrontal cortex is still operating but now it is connected to the direct sensory experiences of the body rather than to the *cowardly self*. In other words, instead of a default state of worry, rumination, and anxiety, mindfulness meditation can move us toward a default state of presence to what is really going on. By waking up to ourselves, we are waking up to reality. By coming home to yourself, you are coming home to the world.

Meditation is not a process of disengagement, as it is often implicitly and explicitly portrayed in both secular and spiritual communities, but rather a process of radical engagement. I love the image presented by the *default mode* research and use it often when talking about meditation and contemplative practices. It helps us to understand the vitally important point that the transforming results of meditation occur not primarily in the practices themselves but in the ways they manifest in normal everyday life. If I base my meditation experience on the yardsticks of "eternal bliss," or achievement of advanced states of boundless love or compassion, then I am a failure. But I am not failing at meditation. Because of it, I am a better father, a better spouse, a better friend, a better colleague, and a better citizen. I make mistakes every single day and I am still around in the muddy messiness of life, but I am aware that my feet are in the mud and I am trying to do it in an aware and decent manner.

As you integrate a perspective of *Wholesome Mindfulness* into your life, you can expect for your default orientation to life to gradually be transformed. The heart-centered approach to life will gradually seep into your messy daily existence. As you come home to yourself, you begin to feel more at home in the world. By now, you may already feel more at home in your body, heart, and emotions. The next step is to extend your awareness and your engagement with *Wholesome Mindfulness* practices into the messiness of the world. You may have recognized that you are more than you thought you were. Now this recognition will be extended to your place in the world.

Connection Through Gratitude

Gratitude and appreciation practices are very powerful ways of tapping into both the goodness of others and how this goodness has benefited us. This type of practice also helps to develop a sense of interconnection to others and to *loosen* our tight sense of self. Appreciation for others and a loosened sense of self go hand in hand. Each reinforces the other. Traditional Tibetan compassion practices go so far as to say that in the cycles of reincarnation, *everyone* has been your mother in a past life (even your worst enemy)! This insight is then coupled with a practice of extending appreciation to each of these mothers who have nurtured and taken care of you. In the following self-reflective activity, you are invited to explore these two dimensions of interconnectedness and appreciation/gratitude.

Self-Reflective Activity: Gratitude

For this journaling exercise, write slowly and deliberately, in the absence of self-judgment, feeling the pencil or pen in your hand or your fingers on the keyboard. Now, take a few deep breaths and calm your mind and prepare for the following journaling activity:

- Reflect back on your life. Pretend you are soaring over your life, taking in all of the events of your life.
- Begin to write down the names of people who have been helpful to you at times in your life.
- Don't censor. Just write down all of the names that occur. It could be people who were helpful to you over long periods. It could be simple individual acts of help and kindness. Just record all of the names that occur to you.
- Now, look over the list.
- Pick one name from the list.
- Write a letter to this person. Include a description of their helpfulness, a description of how this impacted you, and a message of thanks. When you are done, consider imagining the person is there with you and reading your letter out loud to them.
- Return to this exercise again and again, writing letters to others.

Wisdom and Situational Assessment

On your journey home, you are likely to gradually increase your understanding of yourself on several levels, including your values, your potentials, your somatic ground, your mental states, and your genuine capacity for goodness. However, from the perspective of *Wholesome Mindfulness*, the process must also involve an increased ability to bring these qualities into play in the complexities of modern life. Most of us are involved in a complex web of face-to-face and virtual relationships, and the situations in which we live, play, and work are themselves complex and intricate. How can contemplative practices help us to navigate the modern terrain?

How do we engage our journey home with the real lived complexities of daily life? For meditation to be effective it must be much more than a retreat from the actual world. In fact, it must actively engage with it. How do we use the tools of *Wholesome Mindfulness* to accomplish this? We bring the perspective of *Wholesome Mindfulness* into the contexts in which we live. Just as you have now explored tools to help to be able to navigate the context of your internal life, you will now explore tools to help you live more effectively in the world in which you live and have relationships.

I refer to this process as *engaged wisdom*. We sometimes associate wisdom, I think, with an accumulation of knowledge. Here, I use the term more as an ability to be able to see into the nature of things in their complexity. In fact, there is a lot of wisdom in what we have already covered, but it is very self-directed. For example, there is wisdom involved in being able to see the complexity of our emotional experiences. Now, we will extend wisdom and insight into the lived situations of life, a process I refer to as *situational assessment.* It is not enough to bring qualities of calm, focused compassion, and emotional balance into our modern lives (even though this is an amazing accomplishment)! We must be able to understand the physical and virtual situations in which we are embedded. Without this type of understanding, the other qualities are incomplete.

In Tibetan Buddhism, the two main emphases are the development of compassion and wisdom. Either is not complete without the other. Compassion by itself is not enough because it cannot see into the realities of life. Wisdom is not enough because it needs compassion to be fully engaged. Each needs the other. And, there is a tradition known as Mind Training, in which this is done in the context of daily life. The Mind Training tradition brings the insights of meditation into daily life. We have already been doing that through engagement with embodied practices, but now we will take this one step further through the process of *situational assessment.* This involves deepening our understanding of the contexts in which we live. We can then deepen the qualities developed in the previous section of the book through our deepened understanding brought about by *situational assessment,* which essentially encourages us to examine intricacies and interconnections.

Domains of Life

We all have different and overlapping areas in which we live and function. I refer to these as the *domains of life.* I think of these, metaphorically, as spaces. There are large domains of life in which I participate, for instance: work, recreation, family, friendship-based communities, spiritual communities, etc. I can also break these larger domains down into smaller domains and situations. For example, an office meeting is a particular type of situation that occurs for me in the context of a larger domain of work. It can be extremely helpful to pause and reflect and use the insights gleaned from situational assessment to more fully understand the domains of our lives.

The following exercises and contemplations may seem very obvious and simplistic. If so, I encourage you to set this judgment aside and explore these as much as you are willing or able. To me, these practices are where the rubber meets the road, and allow the opportunity to take the path home through *Wholesome Mindfulness* to a new level. In my experience, and for many of my students, some of the most mundane-looking practices are also potentially the most transformational. These practices and reflections offer the opportunity for us to cultivate embodied wisdom and lay the foundation for fully integrating our values and approaches to life that were cultivated in Section 2, and that will be more fully developed in the following chapter.

Self-Reflective Activity: Domains of Life

Take a few deep breaths and calm your mind and prepare for the following journaling activity:

- Reflect on your life. Think of areas or domains of life that are important to you. These are distinct categories representing areas of your life. (Examples: Recreation. Family. Friendships. School/Work. Religious.)
- Make a list of these domains of your life.
- For each domain, identify in ranking order how important they are to you (from one to six, for instance).
- Now, guesstimate what percentage of your waking time is devoted to this domain on a typical week (for example, 20 percent).
- Now, think of one or more core values that are important for you in each domain. You can refer back to the exercise of determining your core values in Chapter 4. For instance, one of my core values in the domain of family might be "trustworthiness." One of my values in career/work might be "competence." These values are a compass that directs us to how we would best like to function and behave in a given domain.
- Pick one domain. Write about why this domain is

important to you, why this value is important to you, and how you can best embody this value.

- If you are comfortable doing this, read this out loud to yourself.
- Now, repeat this exercise for each domain. Write about why each domain is important to you, why this value is important to you, and how you can best embody this value. Then read it out loud to yourself.

The following embodied exercise builds on the foundation that was laid in Chapter 4. The more we are able to operate from the foundation of our inner values, the more purpose and meaning our lives have. Using the tool of situational assessment, this exercise will encourage you to more fully integrate these values into your life.

Embodied Exercise: Embodied Values

This is an embodied activity that can be integrated into daily activities, tapping into your values in the domain where you are present. This practice can help to foster situational awareness, clarity, and purpose.

- Take a moment to calm your mind and center your heart by calmly breathing and reflecting on your inner values.

- Reflect on your current situation. You might even ask yourself, *What situation am I in right now?*
- Just breathe into your situation, taking in as many aspects of it as you can.
- Ask yourself, *What domain of life is this?*
- Now ask yourself, *What value is most important to me here in this situation?*
- As you inhale, breathe in a sense of awareness of this situation.
- As you exhale, breathe out a sense of the value you would like to embody.
- Continue with daily activities, allowing these reflections and to gently ride on the rhythm of the breathing.

Spaces of Communication

Communication today is more layered and complex than ever before in human history. It is very important to bring the tools of situational assessment to this current situation. Moreover, it is changing at a mind-boggling rate and will continue to do so for the foreseeable future. Do you ever feel overwhelmed by emails, texts, social media, and all of the information you juggle? We are bombarded by communication in unprecedented ways. For us not to become insane, and to be able to navigate this terrain with compassion and clarity, it is imperative to be able to bring a perspective of *Wholesome Mindfulness* to what I call the *spaces of communication.* The onslaught of communication is taxing our systems, both personal and social, in new and unpredictable ways. We literally were not wired for this amount of incessant information and must critically examine what is going on, and it begins with each of us individually.

We are assaulted by information (or misinformation) from every direction, and in multiple formats, practically every second of our lives. Moreover, much of the information is not benign. We are either directly or indirectly being persuaded to believe in particular ways with much of the information we take in. Through advertising, we are encouraged to believe things about ourselves and our needs that will propel us to buy goods and services. Through political manipulation we are given messages about what to believe in order to maintain or create power structures. And with the rapid advent and integration of social media into practically every aspect of modern life, it is very difficult to determine the sources of much of the information we are constantly bombarded with. For me, at least, this can easily lead to confusion and anxiety.

I give myself "news fasts" and "social media fasts" in which I do not take in information from these spaces for extended periods, and that offers brief respites, but, I suspect like you, I must use these spaces in some capacity both for my own enjoyment but also by necessity. Thus, it is a constant challenge as to how to use information platforms most effectively. I often daydream about a simpler life that existed in the not-too-distant past, a universe in which the Internet and social media did not exist. For better or worse, it is a reality that will not go away and one that must be navigated with care. To that end, contemplative practices will be key. How can you and I engage most effectively with the information we take in and communicate to others in ways that are informed by wise choices and our deepest values and innate goodness?

A well-meaning email, for instance, can trigger anxiety or anger in me, and if I am not careful, I can unknowingly carry this with me throughout my day. We have seen some of the dangers of the way that reality can be skewed when we are wearing anger or fear goggles, for instance.

It is my belief that contemplative practices can help us to navigate this modern situation effectively. As the old saying goes, knowledge is power. And, in this case, the knowledge emerging from *situational assessment* allows the power to *respond* to the demands of the world from our own intentions and not be caught in an unending cycle of *reactivity.* Understanding the domains of communication in your life will allow you to better manage the information you take in and integrate your values into your communication with others.

Self-Reflective Activity: Domains of Communication

This is a wonderful way to get in touch with the ways we take in and convey information, much of which is often done mindlessly. To prepare for the following journaling exercise, take a few deep breaths and calm your mind.

- Reflect on your life. Think of areas or domains of communication in your life. These are distinct categories of ways you take in and give out information. Be as specific as you can be. (Examples: Email. Social Media. Web Browsing. Television/Streaming Media. Conversation. Texting.) You can do this in the evening as you reflect back on your day.
- Make a list of these domains of communication.
- For each domain, describe *what type* of communication occurred and *how* it occurred.
- You might, for instance, describe that you sent and received emails, or sent and received texts, or browsed the Internet looking for specific information, or browsed the Internet sporadically, or watched the news.
- Now, for each domain of communication, describe choices you had or did not have and the effects of this communication on you. How did it affect you physically? How did it affect you emotionally? How did it affect your thoughts?

Embodied Exercise: Embodied Communication

This is an embodied activity that can be integrated into daily activities in which you are giving and/or receiving information, tapping into your values in the domain where you are present. This practice can help to foster situational awareness, clarity, and purpose.

- Take a moment to calm your mind and center your heart by calmly breathing and reflecting on your inner values.
- Reflect on your current situation. You might even ask yourself, *What situation am I in right now?* Now ask, *What space(s) of communication am I engaged in?*
- Just breathe into your situation, taking in as many aspects of it as you can.
- Ask yourself, *Can I choose whether to communicate or not?*
- *What is my motivation right now?*
- *Does this motivation match my inner values?*
- *What emotional lens am I seeing the world through right now?*
- Now return to your communication and engage as mindfully as you can, embodying your core values.

Please note that if you would like additional reflective activities, embodied exercises, and a guided meditation on this topic, more are accessible at the book's resource page: www.dentgitchel.com/pursuingpurpose.

Embodying Wholesome Mindfulness

Even if our heart is open and our values are intact, we can still have great difficulty understanding the actual situations in which we live. If we wake up a bit—and loosen our perspective—and allow our wisdom to emerge, a much more nuanced and realistic perspective also emerges. It is at this point that compassion and empathy for others can begin to blossom more fully, and it further sets the stage for the further extension of heart practices in the next chapter.

The flip side of this is that you might continue to gain a more spacious, flexible, and nuanced understanding of yourself. You might have noticed this after reading about and exploring the domains of life offered above. In my experience, any time we can loosen up and understand our self with a little more context—a little more nuance—then we are better able to successfully navigate the challenges offered by life and to live more consistently with the internal values and heart-centered motivations that have been cultivated through the process of *Wholesome Mindfulness*. The more you can clearly and accurately understand the life situations in which you are embedded and which you participate, the more you are able to flourish.

For instance, suppose I am about to enter a meeting at work. Typically, I might do so from a state of relative mindlessness. Sure, I am aware at some level this is work and this is a meeting for such and such reason and that certain people will be there. But I am likely operating largely on autopilot. I have done this so many times that I can just walk in and deal with whatever occurs. Traditional approaches to mindfulness might help me by offering tools to be more aware of my sensations, thoughts, and emotions while in the meeting. But it is still *my* processes that I am aware of. While this approach is no doubt helpful (and not easy to implement!), it is not able to capture the intricacies and complexities of modern life.

If I expand my critical intelligence to encompass the entire situation before entering the meeting, I might reflect on questions such as: What are the values and purpose of the meeting, from the perspective of the organization? Who else will be in the meeting other than myself? What is it like to reflect on each of them *individually* and to reflect that, *just like me*, each has her own values and habitual emotional reactions that they are bringing to the table? What values—and subsequent behaviors—would I like to best embody in my interactions with others? What habitual reactions of mine will likely be triggered during the meeting? In other words, the more I am able to *understand* the situation at hand, the better I am able to embody my *courageous self*.

In my experiences, my *cowardly self* is easily triggered in stressful situations. Once this occurs, I can easily become hijacked by my reactionary emotional patterns, retreat into worry and anxiety, become divorced from my inner values, and fail to see the bigger picture. Just as in the case with mindfulness of breathing practice, the practice here is the same: Recognize. Relax. Release. Return. I recognize that my best intentions have been hijacked. I relax my body and mind. I release, as much as possible, my overattachment to whatever emotional hijacking has occurred. And I return to *embodied contextual awareness.* From the perspective offered, here meditation and contextual practices are ultimately not about feeling better (though this is important), but about being able to live and breathe more skillfully and effectively from a heart-centered and value-laden perspective in the actual messy situations of life.

Please note that all self-reflective activities, guided meditations, and embodied exercises in the book, along with bonus activities, are accessible at the book's resource page: www.dentgitchel.com/pursuingpurpose

Chapter 8

Embodied Compassion

In the last chapter, we worked on extending our contemplative practices into the complex modern world in which we live. Now, we will build on that and work on cultivating qualities of our inner goodness, innate compassion, and unconditional kindness, and infusing them into all our interactions. This is what I need to flourish. This is what you need to flourish. This is what the world needs to sustain and flourish.

Compassion as Strength

Compassion is not weakness. You may experience this directly through your practice of *Wholesome Mindfulness*. This goes against popular views of compassion. As for myself, after many years of working with compassion practice, I still resist this notion at times. However, through my own experience, and those of mentors and students, I can verify that I now firmly believe this. But, how can this be so? How can being with difficulty and suffering give us strength? Well, it depends on *how* we do this. Through the practice of compassion cultivation, we learn *how* to be with suffering a new and different way. This, of course, like everything else is a process and one that gradually emerges and strengthens over time. But it is real, and it is time-tested.

In Tibet, material progress was not valued at all, but following from the ancient Indian Buddhist culture, which they largely absorbed, a "contemplative laboratory" of sorts was developed and sustained for many hundreds of years. Just as the Western world developed sophisticated methods for observing and measuring the external world, Tibetan Buddhism did the same for the internal world. Just as the Western world was able to progress in knowledge due to the development and testing of hypotheses, Tibetan Buddhism was able to progress in its methods of understanding and developing our deepest human capacities. And perhaps the deepest of these are the qualities of our innate goodness, compassion, and unconditional kindness. In the contemplative laboratories of Tibet, methods for accessing and cultivating these qualities were developed, refined, and time-tested. And fortunately, the Great Compassion Tradition of Tibet has been made available to the modern world.

Our normal and habitual responses to suffering are to turn away from it or to feel overwhelmed by it. For instance, when encountering a homeless person, I may experience distress and be overcome by it. However, to defend myself from this reaction, I may also develop an ability to completely ignore the suffering and thus to shield myself from distress. Unless something great is at stake, we are unlikely to willingly open ourselves to difficulty. For various reasons, most of us have learned that to be vulnerable is to open ourselves to hurt and we have developed magnificent coping strategies to resist this. We are actually masters at this! It protects us and gives us strength of sorts, but this resistance takes us further away from our values and our innate goodness and courage. There is no blame in this. Each of us has learned various survival skills, and for most of us, resisting pain and suffering is likely one of them.

There is a strength and nobility in fully developed compassion that is unfathomable and difficult to grasp for those of us raised in a culture that is largely emotionally illiterate and unaware of our innate goodness. I have witnessed it up close. My friend and mentor, Geshe Thupten Dorjee, is a refugee, forced to flee by foot from his homeland in Tibet as a young child over the mountains to India. Many died on the journey. He was then raised in poverty in refugee camps and later in a monastery. He came to the United States as a middle-aged adult who did not know English and has persevered and has taught and lived here now for 20 years. His strength, to me, is almost unimaginable. He has integrated into the local community and teaches and offers services to others with a passion and commitment I have never before witnessed, all the while in a foreign culture using a language he learned on his own and with no translator. He nurtures and teaches us who have so much while his family and culture of origin live far away in a situation of exile or occupation, all the while doing so with dignity, compassion, and strength.

And, his situation is not unique. Students at the University of Arkansas, under the guidance of Geshe Thupten Dorjee and Dr. Sidney Burris, have visited Tibetans living in exile in India and have compiled their stories through an oral history project. What comes out in these stories is the same strength, dignity, and compassion demonstrated by Geshe. There are accounts of Tibetans who have been imprisoned and tortured for decades who come out of this with their compassion for humanity intact. Tibetans experience trauma due to horrific situations just like others do. But there is a strength and courage in this culture that is undeniable. And, to me, it is largely due to the Great Compassion Tradition. It gives me hope in the human condition and faith in human goodness, strength, and resilience. And importantly, *these qualities can be trained.*

We have many misconceptions about compassion. We may think of it as taking in the suffering of others. We may think of it as feeling sorry for others. We may think of it as sacrificing our own needs for the needs of others. We may think of it as a strong reactive emotion. All of these are wrong. When true compassion is cultivated, what emerges is wisdom, strength, and resilience. Through the cultivation of compassion, you can gradually awaken to the birthright of your own dignified human existence. Each small step that you cultivate compassion on the path of *Wholesome Mindfulness* will result in more meaning and purpose in your life. Compassion cultivation is not only for exceptional beings and advanced meditators but is for us all. The more we cultivate and live our lives through the lens of compassion, the more we are able to be decent human beings.

Compassion as Embodied Wisdom

Part of the strength of compassion is that it is the embodiment of wisdom. Through the lens of compassion, we better *understand* and respond to both the needs of others and ourselves. The inclination to compassionate action is instinctual and innate to all of us. We are simply taking this innate instinct and exercising it and allowing it to grow. Unless we have been conditioned otherwise, we naturally gravitate toward service and assistance to those in need. This can perhaps best be observed with a parent and young child. There is a natural capacity to care and comfort, and strength and courage effortlessly emerge to face any difficulty in the service of the needs of the child. Or think of natural disasters or other large-scale calamities. The strength and courage automatically come on display as this natural instinct for compassion is triggered. However, this modern instinct is very limited in its application and is not fully suited for the requirements of modern life. It is limited largely to times of crisis or to those whom we have a strong emotional bond.

Typically, the *cowardly self*, out of fear and self-protection, puts people in boxes and evaluates their worth through the lenses of reactive emotions and stereotypes. We may experience some individuals as likable. These are people in our "in group," so to speak. There are people that we perceive as similar to us, or similar to how we think we are or would like to be, according to stories we have spun in our minds and the reactive emotional patterns that are ties to these stories. Those in our "in group" are likely to receive a compassionate response when they are undergoing suffering, and this is what we seemed to be biologically wired to do. Even when we are living from the *cowardly self* and our contemplative awareness is undeveloped, spontaneous and pure compassion can burst through. But it is limited and unsustainable.

The selectivity of instinctual compassion, and our noncompassionate responses, is our evolutionary inheritance. It is normal. As one of my mentors has sometimes said, when these occur "the brain is just doing what the brain does." Fortunately, however, this is not the last word. Through training we can change our brains, and thus, our reactions to the suffering of others. The Great Compassion Tradition coming out of the "contemplative laboratory" of Tibet, as well as current scientific research, demonstrates this fact. We can alter our evolutionary inheritance and become less reactionary and more authentic, kind, and compassionate across the board. We can then be better people and citizens. And, this is not a religious exercise. It is, rather, an endeavor of embodying our decency. It is open to anyone and everyone. It is open to me. It is open to you. Your authenticity depends on it. My authenticity depends on it. The practices of *Wholesome Mindfulness* can help you to dip your toes into the water of the Great Compassion Tradition and help to bring meaning and purpose to your life. Your compassion can expand and allow you to more effectively provide service both to yourself and those around you.

Overcoming Misconceptions About Compassion

Compassion leads to happiness. This, my friend, is counter-intuitive and typically evokes resistance in people. It is not uncommon for students to report with surprise that compassion meditation causes them to feel good. This is often quite surprising and challenges their conventional notions of compassion. When I first begin to deeply immerse myself in compassion practices daily, I was amazed at how I often felt open, spacious, and content at the end of my meditation session. During the practice, I often felt resistance, or "nothing," like I was going through the motions, and then at the end this more expansive and spacious state would often emerge.

This is not the transitory and unsustainable form of happiness we associate with thrill, excitement, or the rush of pleasure. Rather, it is a form of happiness that is sustainable and grounded in contentment resulting from living a life of purpose and meaning in accordance with our deepest values. As you come increasingly into contact with this form of happiness, you may recognize that its depth and authenticity are much greater than the transitory forms of happiness you have experienced before.

When speaking of compassion, I often like to say that "it is not an emotion." On one level, this is probably intended to startle people a bit and to encourage them to listen and think. But, on a deeper level, it is something I believe wholeheartedly and that helps to distinguish traditional understandings of compassion from the type of compassion that is cultivated and strengthened through meditation practices. Whereas the former may be thought of as a reactive emotion, the compassion that is trained can become a state of being that can infuse all aspects of life.

Compassion Can Be Broadened and Extended

Through training, compassion can be broadened and extended. This was alluded to above but needs to be explicitly restated and reinforced. The habitual boxes we put others into based on conscious and unconscious assumptions and biases can be gradually overcome. Many, including prominent scientists, are skeptical of this claim, and you might be as well.

This skepticism is natural but the conclusions that it draws are not correct. The Great Compassion Tradition of Tibet and modern scientific research demonstrates the effects of compassion cultivation. The brain changes—and our experiences change—as our cultivation of compassion increases. The noted evolutionary psychologist Paul Eckman was notoriously skeptical of the idea of broadening compassion until he came into close contact and dialogue with His Holiness the Dalai Lama, a modern exemplar of the Great Compassion Tradition, and is now a public advocate of global compassion.

I like to reframe compassion in terms of the *default network* idea that was presented earlier. If you recall, this is your brain's baseline state, how it functions normally when you are not doing anything else. It has been shown to change through the practice of mindfulness meditation. Through compassion practice, our default state of mind to life itself can become transformed. When wearing compassion goggles, we can see the world clearly and notice our kinship to humanity, and ultimately, all of life itself. We can encounter strangers through the lens of commonality rather than through the lens of difference. This is not to say that difference does not exist or should not be celebrated. But, when difference is seen at the *perceptual* level, through the lenses of reactive emotions, the differences are seen as threats at worst and simply as nuisances at best, and the *cowardly self* is fully in charge. However, when similarity and kinship are seen at the *perceptual* level, through the unbiased lens of compassion, differences are not seen as threats and are celebrated. This is the state of mind that compassion engenders. I think of it as our optimal evolutionary goal. It is the default state that we all should strive for, regardless of our particular religious or cultural affiliation. It is up to each of us whether this occurs or not. No one is a bystander.

Situational Assessment and Even-Mindedness: A Practical Approach

An important step in the process of developing compassion is to extend the mindset of *situational assessment* into the world of personal and community relationships. As we have seen, we have many deeply held ingrained biases that tend to prevent our ability to see others accurately and to respond to them with unconditional kindness and compassion. Triggered by our unconscious biases, assumptions, and deeply held stereotypes, we are often seeing others through the lenses of our projections and emotional reactions.

As we extend *situational assessment* into the world of humanity, a critical step is made. As we reflect on the others that we encounter in our relationships and in our communities, we begin to sense *similarities* that exist between others and ourselves. This is an important and foundational step in the cultivation of compassion. In fact, without this step, compassion cannot be enhanced to its fullest potential.

This quality that emerges can be called *even-mindedness*. In traditional meditations of the Great Compassion Tradition, the others that we reflect upon are typically divided into three categories: those we are attached to (in group); those who are irrelevant to us, or we are indifferent to; and those we have an aversion toward (out group). By reflecting time and again on the similarity between oneself and those representing these three categories, some of our habitual psychological and emotional barriers begin to soften a bit and *even-mindedness* begins to emerge. When I first began to delve deeply into this, I coined the phrase *cool compassion* for this state of mind. For me, it sometimes has had the feeling of a cool breeze on my skin on a warm sunny day. It is soothing and relaxing and allows me to relax a bit and be a little less on guard. It has a distinctive feeling of *softening*. Through this practice, your assumptions and stereotypes of others will be gradually softened.

Once a stable experience of *even-mindedness* is achieved, this is extended to e*veryone*. In my own practice experiences and in teaching others, I have found this globalizing effort (to everyone) to be a strong barrier. Many of us are so perfectionistic (even if we do not realize it) and so hard on ourselves (even if we do not realize it), that a sense of frustration or self-judgment often emerges. Our minds often tend to jump to political leaders or public figures or groups of people who have committed atrocities, and then to determine that this process is not something that should be undertaken or that it is impossible.

This is not what is being asked or expected. My initial advice to everyone is to work with the actual situations in your own life. It is here where the rubber meets the road. And it is here that your practice will gain traction. *Soften the edges and begin with the people who you encounter in your actual life and work only with those who are workable for you.* This will have enormous benefits in your life and as your edges become gradually softened. By integrating the reflections of *even-mindedness* into your mindset of *situational assessment,* you can gain more clarity and evenness in your human interactions and can expect for this state of mind to spontaneously seep into your life in unexpected ways. The following exercises on *even-mindedness* are fairly straightforward and easy but can be extremely transformative.

Self-Reflective Activity: Cultivating Even-Mindedness

Take a few deep breaths and calm your mind and prepare for the following journaling activity:

- Make a separate page for each of four categories: Compassion, Pity, Disdain, and Disgust.
- On the sheet titled "Compassion," make a list of people *in your life* who you have positive feelings for and that, on a very basic level, you see as relatively equal to yourself in worth. These can be friends, respected colleagues, or anyone who you would tend

to have compassion for if they were suffering. Please also include here any stereotypes that might trigger a compassion response in you.

- Be creative in this process and do not overly self-criticize.
- On the sheet titled "Pity," make a list of people *in your life* who you have positive feelings for but that, on a very basic level, you see as "lower" than yourself. Here, the dominant instinctual response if they were suffering might be pity. Please also include here any stereotypes that might trigger a pity response in you. Try to be as honest with yourself as you can, with no self-judgment.
- On the sheet titled "Disdain," make a list of people *in your life* who you have negative feelings for and that, on a very basic level, you see as powerful in some way. Here, the dominant instinctual response if they were suffering might be disdain or even a subtle enjoyment. There is satisfaction knowing they "deserve it." Please also include any stereotypes that might trigger this response in you (such as political affiliation, etc.). Try to be as honest with yourself as you can, with no self-judgment.
- On the sheet titled "Disgust," make a list of people *in your life* who you have negative feelings for and that, on a very basic level, you see as "less than yourself."

Here, the dominant instinctual response if they were suffering might be disgust, or you might dismiss it completely. These might be people who trigger disgust in you when you see them, or maybe trigger a response of looking away so they are and "invisible" of sorts. Please also include here any stereotypes that might trigger this response in you. Try to be as honest with yourself as you can, with no self-judgment.

- Now, just sit for a few moments and allow what you have reflected on to sink in.
- Write down any observations you have of this experience: *What were you feeling as you did this activity? What are you feeling in your body and in your emotional mind now?*
- Reflect on the fact that you do not view everyone in the same way and that the boxes you put people in affect how you respond to them emotionally.
- Recognize that this is part of our biological inheritance and that *everyone* does this.

Embodied Exercise:
Embodied Contextual Even-Mindedness

This is an embodied activity that can be integrated into daily activities, helping you to see others through the lens of *even-mindedness*.

- Take a moment to calm your mind and center your heart by calmly breathing and reflecting on your inner values.
- Reflect on your current situation. Reflect on others who you have recently interacted with, or whom you likely will interact with.
- Just breathe into your situation, taking in as many aspects of it as you can.
- Breathe into the fact that you all share basic human impulses and conditioning. You all have deep inner values. You all have innate inner goodness and communities to which you belong. At a very basic level, you all share a deep human kinship.
- As you inhale, breathe in a sense of connection with others silently reciting, "Like me, each of us suffers."
- As you exhale, solidify this recognition by silently reciting, "Like me, each of us has joys."
- Continue with daily activities, allowing these reflections, and to gently ride on the rhythm of the breathing and imagining your similarity to others.

Broadening Compassion

As His Holiness the Dalai Lama often says, compassion is basically dependent on a feeling of kinship, or at least of similarity, and in cultivating compassion we extend this feeling of kinship or similarity to wider circles of people. Basically, we take the mindset of *even-mindedness* and use this as the foundation for growing our compassion. This is a natural and logical step. As your *even-mindedness* becomes more stable and your edges become softer, it is quite natural to begin to extend compassion more broadly in the situations in which you live, breathe, and work. In the practices of broadening and extending compassion we put a little fuel on the fire *even-mindedness* to enhance this natural process.

This type of compassion has not been valued, or even thought possible, in the modern world. If compassion is seen as just one among a host of reactive emotions, and our emotions are thought to be hardwired, then it makes no sense to think that reactive compassion can be broadened into a more expansive form of compassion. Yet, it can. The brain, and its experiences, are malleable and this is *good news.* Our brains are constantly in flux. We have a choice to make. Do we go down the road of tribalism and the *cowardly self,* or do we go down the road of expansive compassion and the *courageous self?* I choose the latter. How about you?

Below is an exercise to help you to embody expansive compassion in the grind of daily life.

Embodied Exercise: Embodied Expansive Compassion

This is an embodied activity that can be integrated into daily activities, tapping into your innate compassion and using this to fuel an attitude of strength and compassion.

- Take a moment and calm your mind and center your heart by calmly breathing and reflecting on your inner values.
- Reflect on your current situation.
- Just breathe into your situation, taking in as many aspects of it as you can.
- Breathe into your heart and get in touch with your innate strength and compassion.
- Ask yourself, *What difficulty are you aware of? How does this affect you in your body as you reflect on this?*
- As you inhale, breathe in a sense of awareness of your current situation and a sense that you can be present to any difficulties, or suffering, that is present. For instance, if I am washing the dishes, I can be aware of water shortages and the fact that some people do not have adequate fresh water. I can be aware of my feelings of distress, sadness, or guilt that arise. I can hold all of these layers in my attention as I inhale.
- Recall that everyone you interact with, just like yourself, shares a common biological inheritance.

Everyone you interact with struggles with modern life and experiences emotional upheavals. Just like you, everyone you interact with has deep inner values, loved ones, and friends.

- As you exhale, breathe out a sense of spreading compassion to yourself and others, reciting silently in your mind, "May each of us be free of suffering and difficulty."
- Continue with daily activities, allowing these reflections, and to gently ride on the rhythm of the breathing and imagine sending out your compassion to yourself and to others as you continue.
- Be creative. Imagine that your compassion is effective and providing relief. You might, for instance, imagine that everyone has access to clean water, or that we have emotional healing.

Sustainability and a One-World Perspective

Compassion, from this perspective, is ultimately about a one-world perspective. This perspective is a natural product of the compassion cultivation process. As your edges become softened, it is highly likely that your notions of citizenship and group affiliation will change as well. This is the wholesome perspective toward which every authentic world tradition—religious and secular—points ultimately. We will feel a sense of kinship with everyone, a *planetary consciousness*. All other "isms," such as racism and sexism, will be seen as the fearful projections of the *cowardly self* that they in actuality are. They may have served us in greater or lesser degrees in the past, but their time and usefulness are outdated. Compassion is our evolutionary inheritance, at least if we want to survive and flourish.

Once a perspective of compassion is instilled in your heart and mind, it cannot be taken away by arguments, memes, or force. It, of course, will be challenged. It is a process, and that is never at completion. I still make mistakes every day. I yell at my spouse. I get aggravated at a coworker and feel in my heart that he is aggravating at his very core, that this defines him. I believe that people who are ignorant or commit horrible atrocities are basically unredeemable. But when I pause and come back to my core and access what compassion I might have, I recognize my mistakes and resoften these edges through the cool nourishment of meditation and reflective contemplations. Compassion is a process without an end, and by softening our edges we can come back to our own innate goodness and compassion for others again and again. We then tap into our true evolutionary inheritance: a sense of kinship with everyone and a strong conviction that *We. Are. In. This. Together.* I am in. Are you? Let's not let the *lizard brain* prevail. I've got this. You've got this. We've got this. *We. Are. All. In. This. Together.*

Picture a bright blue ball just spinning, spinning free
Dizzy with eternity
Paint it with a skin of sky, brush in some clouds and sea
Call it home for you and me
A peaceful place, or so it looks from space
A closer look reveals the human race
Full of hope, full of grace, is the human face
But afraid we may lay it all to waste

—Grateful Dead

Please note that all self-reflective activities, guided meditations, and embodied exercises in the book, along with bonus activities, are accessible at the book's resource page: www.dentgitchel.com/pursuingpurpose.

CHAPTER 9

Moving Forward

Where do you go from here? The practices and perspectives of *Wholesome Mindfulness* presented in this book are not linear. There is a certain development process in the presentation, but the lived process is not linear and stepwise. Life is not linear, and neither are the processes of personal development and the journey of coming home. We proceed in steps but then return to the foundational steps again and again. In my experiences, the practices and perspectives presented in this book have infinite layers.

Engaging in the practices of *Wholesome Mindfulness* is an ongoing process, and I continue to return to my values daily, and refine them, in the swirl of busy modern life. I formally return to my body *every single day* and, to me, that is the foundation of every other practice. I have to breathe into my innate goodness *every* chance I get to ward off forgetfulness and fear. I have to watch my emotional mind like a hawk to remain balanced and on point. I have to tap into what wisdom I have acquired and look into the complex situations of life and into the spaces that I live and communicate, or else get overwhelmed by the ongoing pressures of modernity. I must work on developing my compassion and *even-mindedness* as if my life depends on it, because it does.

These processes are ongoing, but they continue to uncover deeper levels of meaning and purpose. The journey home is never complete, but it becomes increasingly profound. There is a bit of a paradox in all of this. On one level, the journey takes a lot of effort. But, on another level, it is one of discovery. We put in a lot of work and effort, but in a sense, what we are cultivating is already there. In my experience, the path home begins to become more familiar and natural and less contrived. We put in work and discover what was already there.

Returning home is a journey through the mud of our minds and social expectations. It takes constant discernment to know what to do, how much of it to do, and when to do it. No one but you can do it. Friends can point the way, point out a tip or two and maybe even provide directions, but only you take your journey home. Yet, progress is made. Of that I am sure. And with progress comes more insight and more tools. At every step of the journey home you know a little more about yourself and of the world you inhabit, and with that comes more choice about what to do with this awareness. It takes discernment and a scientific mindset to know what tools to use and when, but that is part of the progress that occurs in the process of coming home.

For instance, I may notice that I am experiencing a strong reactive emotion, one that tends to knock me off balance and return me to my *cowardly self.* I have several tools at my disposal: I can breathe into my inner values and see if I am being led astray. I can return to my body and feel my groundedness and experience what is going on in a direct way to avoid being taken away by rumination and that whole mental trip. I can utilize self-compassion and generate compassion for myself, and then for others experiencing similar difficulties. I have found that this latter method is effective for me in public settings, such as before a speaking engagement when my little inner introvert tries to show up and sabotage. It allows me to get out of my scared self, who gets constricted and alone, and to connect with my goodness and those around me. With insight I can choose which tool to implement.

As you gain familiarity with the tools of *Wholesome Mindfulness*, you develop more flexibility, adaptability, and resilience to meet the complex challenges of modern life. Formal practice, in my opinion, is indispensable and lays the foundation for this, but the ultimate goal is to be able to deal effectively, wisely, and compassionately with the messiness of embodied life. And it is a solitary process. Yet, as you do your own work, you also foster more meaningful connections with others.

As you connect to your own heart, you also connect to the goodness and the hearts of those around you. Your life turns into a life of service to who you really are, and this inevitably involves serving communities. You recognize this logic intuitively and do what needs to be done just because.

Identity

Little by little, the path of *Wholesome Mindfulness* brings us into contact with the ingrained habits, thoughts, and emotions of our identities, and as such, these identities themselves are transformed.

Each of us must use the compass of our own critical awareness to determine what direction we are sailing and to make adjustments as needed. Identifies are always in flux and, as such, are consistently being transformed on the contemplative path. For instance, recognizing a particular reactive emotional pattern and trying to bring compassionate awareness to it is not likely to be an easy process. This pattern has likely been around for a *very long time* and is very much part of self-identity. Bringing awareness to it and trying to become less attached to it may be threatening on many levels.

I have been undergoing an identity transformation while writing this book. I have been trained in academia, and academia has particular ways of writing and conducting research that is deemed as "legitimate," and there are many hierarchies embedded in this. My identity that I have cultivated over the past 13 years or so has been subtly spun around the explicit and implicit expectations of what is required to be "successful" in academia. As this book was conceived and began to emerge, I have become increasingly aware that it threatens many of these assumptions and has brought to the fore many resistances and strong emotions. This book is written from my heart and is intended to be a friend to you on your path. And, in that, it has been threatening to my academic self-identity.

What will experts think of this book? I do not have enough footnotes and references for this to be a legitimate book. Who am I to be writing such a book? What will people think of me if I disclose my own weaknesses and struggles? Am I destroying my academic career in writing this? These are the types of thoughts that I have been bombarded with, and I have had to work my way through strong emotions amid all of this. I have come to realize that I have subtly spun a very strong narrative of what it means to be successful in academia and this particular book has been very threatening to that.

And yet, I have persisted. Why? I have done so because of my values and, ultimately, the deeper purpose these values have helped to uncover and manifest: to help others find their way home. By tapping into my own inner values, something that is a constant and unfolding process, this book has naturally emerged. I have come to see the self-doubt, self-criticisms, and strong emotions that have emerged as resulting in my self-identity being threatened, and that process, transformed. In any growth process, we come out the other side transformed in some ways, and such a transformation involves changes in self-identity. In constructing new narratives, old narratives die or are altered and there are inherent challenges in this process. Go easy on yourself. Be compassionate with yourself. Hold on to your values and move forward but do this lightly and kindly.

Community

As we deepen and transform our relationship with ourselves, we are getting healthier than ever and have the power and tools to transform the entire planet into a beautiful and sustainable community—one community full of love, respect, and purpose. This may seem like a distant fantasy, but it is so close and available. The key is to take off our lenses of delusion and fear and come home. Just look around with clear vision and come home. Look at yourself. Look at the world. When you see your own innermost values, you see the innermost values of the world. When you see your heart, you see the heart of the world. When you come home to yourself, you come home to us all. We are all in this together. All we have to do to look and see. The solitary journey of coming home is thus a journey back into the true community of life. When community is approached from the mindset of the *Wholesome Mindfulness,* then community is sustaining and life-affirming.

For many of us, our experiences of community have not been life- and value-affirming. Sure, we might have a long series of friendships and family relations, etc., and yet, something may seem missing. From the lens of compassion, we begin to seek communities of others who share like-minded visions. When recognizing our own goodness and experiencing the world through the perspective of our *courageous self,* it is necessary and healthy to seek companionships that overlap with our new and deepening understanding of life. As you come to your heart, to your self, you come home to like-minded friends and communities along the way. It is a solitary journey in many ways, but it is also one that can be shared with others in deep and intimate connections.

Today I am blessed to be a member of several loving and supportive communities. Communities don't have to be formal or explicitly spiritual, but I think it is very important to be part of supportive communities. Particularly in the modern world, the contemplative path must involve significant engagement with messy complexities and, as such, it is important to have a strong foundation on which to stand. Community provides such a foundation, and there are many types of communities. Today, in the modern world, we are lonelier than ever, but we also have more opportunities than ever to forge new types of communities of the heart. Compassion is ultimately about connection based on shared common humanity and, as such, it calls us to innovative forms of community that allow us to flourish and meet the challenges of the rapidly changing modern world. True community involves friendships of the heart and I hope this book can serve as a friend to you. There are also additional resources and opportunities for continued growth and community available on the website.

Coming Home as a Process

Coming home is a process and you will never reach a final destination. However, as you progress, your internal compass will become stronger and stronger. You will not necessarily know where the path or journey is headed, but you will *know* you are headed in the right direction. Of course, you will lose your way at times; at least, I do. But, from coming home to or redefining my inner values or connecting with a trusted friend, I am able to recalibrate my compass and proceed. It is not always smooth, but it is necessary, and always results in deeper levels of happiness and meaning. Trust your inner barometer and allow your path to unfold in ways that best embody your heart and your values.

Many Paths

There are as many paths as there are individuals. What is important is that each of us finds our own path, one that embraces our shared common humanity. The perspective and practices of *Wholesome Mindfulness* are intended to be malleable and flexible and adaptable to multiple paths. We must move beyond “isms.” We must steer our evolutionary heritage toward compassion, justice, and sustainability. By recognizing our innate similarities, we can then celebrate our magnificent diversity. With wisdom and compassion as our guides, we can approach worldwide human flourishing and maximize our evolutionary potential. In a sense, many paths can become one path—one of kindness, respect, and cooperation.

This may seem naïve but what makes it enticing is that it is true. Waking up and coming home is about being aware, and awareness is about seeing things as they truly are and embodying this in our hearts and actions. Through the lenses of reactive emotions, we have not seen things correctly, and this has resulted in the strife, division, and cruelty that we see around us. But this is all based on delusion. With courage and strength, it is possible to wake up and see things clearly. For instance, when you wake up to your own innate goodness, there is a natural recognition that this exists in everyone else. When you have compassion for your own reactive emotions, you develop compassion for others who are enslaved by their own reactive emotions. When you come to your heart and your own path home, you come home to the realization that everyone has their own unique path home. Waking up to the deep reality of connection is to wake up to the celebration of many paths based on an immense love stemming from a sense of kinship. To celebrate your path is to celebrate every path.

There is a road, no simple highway
Between the dawn and the dark of night
And if you go no one may follow,
That path is for your steps alone

—Robert Hunter / Grateful Dead

Please note that all self-reflective activities, guided meditations, and embodied exercises in the book, along with bonus activities, are accessible at the book's resource page: www.dentgitchel.com/pursuingpurpose.

About the Author

Dent Gitchel, Jr.

Dent Gitchel is a meditation teacher, clinician, and researcher. He has 30 years of experience as a meditation practitioner and has been teaching meditation for the past decade. Though his main teachers have been Tibetan Buddhists, he has studied with a wide range of religious and secular teachers. He was one of the first certified teachers of Stanford's *Compassion Cultivation Training* and was also in the teacher training program for *Mindfulness Based Emotional Balance.* He regularly teaches classes and workshops and has taught in a wide variety of secular and religious settings. He has a doctorate in Rehabilitation Education and Research and is trained as both a Rehabilitation Counselor and a Licensed Associate Counselor. He was selected three times as a *Senior Investigator* at the *Mind and Life Summer Research Institute* and has presented at many national and international conferences.

He was born and raised in Little Rock, Arkansas, and lives there with his wife, Shannon, and children, Henry and Lilah. He loves spending time outdoors, especially hiking and camping. Though not a formal musician, he loves attending live concerts and has attended well over 100 Grateful Dead concerts! A favorite day would include hiking through the Ozark Mountains with his family.

Acknowledgments

This book is basically a product of all of my experiences and, as such, there are literally thousands who participated in this journey. As I scan my life, I am thankful to have had so many influential relationships.

Initial thanks go out to Catherine Gregory and Modern Wisdom Press. Her guidance through the writing and editing process has been invaluable and this book would not have come to fruition without her.

My primary sense of appreciation goes out to my wife, Shannon, and my children, Lilah and Henry. It is not an exaggeration to say you have taught me more about love than anything else in my life. Because of you, I have grown in ways I could never have imagined.

I would like to thank my parents, brother, and extended family. You have sown the seeds in me of tolerance and curiosity and encouraged me to pursue my own path.

Since childhood, I have been fortunate to have many friendships, and scanning my life, I am deeply appreciative of the gifts I have received from these supportive connections.

I would like to express special thanks to the many wonderful teachers I have encountered over the years. Particularly, my deepest gratitude is extended toward those who opened to me the world of meditation and Buddhism: Dr. Jay McDaniel, Lama Yeshe Wangmo, Dr. Anne Klein, Dr. Harvey Aronson, and Margaret Cullen. Without them, I would not have acquired even the little amount of knowledge I do have.

Primary among my teachers is Geshe Thupten Dorjee. I was fortunate enough to have met him when he first came to teach in Arkansas in August, 2006, and have been a friend and student since. Through him, I realized that mediation is not something you simply do, another activity to fit into our busy schedule, but rather, it is a way of living and a mindset toward living that should permeate everything we do. Geshe-la helped me to assimilate many important concepts and teachings but, most importantly, he models a contemplative and ethical perspective toward life in all he does. May the Great Compassion Tradition of Tibet long flourish.

Thank You

Thank you, dear friend, for accompanying me on this journey. The process of writing this book was very transformational for me, and I hope the information and tools here have been meaningful for you. This book is very much the book I would have loved to receive many years ago.

Please reach out to me to let me know your feedback. You can learn more about my workshops and online offerings at www.dentgitchel.com. Whatever your path in life, my deepest wish is that you have found something in these pages that will help to nourish you on your journey.

www.ingramcontent.com/pod-product-compliance
Lightning Source LLC
LaVergne TN
LVHW041316080426
835513LV00008B/485